BREAKNECK

The Early Settlement of Middlebury, Connecticut: From 1657 to its Incorporation as a Town.

RAYMOND E. SULLIVAN

iUniverse, Inc.
New York   Bloomington

BREAKNECK
The Early Settlement of Middlebury, Connecticut:
From 1657 to its Incorporation as a Town.

iUniverse books may be ordered through booksellers or by contacting:

*iUniverse
1663 Liberty Drive
Bloomington, IN 47403
www.iuniverse.com
1-800-Authors (1-800-288-4677)*

*Because of the dynamic nature of the Internet, any Web addresses or links contained in this book
may have changed since publication and may no longer be valid. The views expressed in this work
are solely those of the author and do not necessarily reflect the views of the publisher, and the
publisher hereby disclaims any responsibility for them.*

*ISBN: 978-1-4502-5632-2 (pbk)
ISBN: 978-1-4502-5633-9 (ebk)*

Printed in the United States of America

iUniverse rev. date: 10/6/10

A Dedication

To the many lost souls, the founders of Middlebury, who lay buried in the cold, rich earth at Breakneck, in long ignored and unmarked graves. May they all rest in eternal peace!

Acknowledgments

The Author is indebted firstly to Henry Bronson, MD and to Joseph Anderson, DD for their outstanding efforts in chronicling the history of Waterbury, Connecticut's ancient past. Others, as noted in the Forward to this volume, have contributed much to our knowledge of West Farms and the settlement of Breakneck, in particular.

Special thanks must go to Edith Salisbury, Middlebury's Town Clerk and her Assistant Town Clerk, Brigitte Bessette, for their generous help in researching owners of the land, which makes up the area called Breakneck. Appreciation is also due to Jane Gallagher, Chief Librarian, Middlebury Public Library, for reviewing this manuscript and offering substantive suggestions of improvement. Our thanks, as well, to Michelle Berthiaume of Shutter Speed Photo, in Middlebury, for assistance with the photo images in this work, Joseph DeSantis for his advice on the archaeology of the area, to Jessica Stiles, Editorial Consultant and to Jade Council, Publishing Services Associate at iUniverse for her patience and assistance with this manuscript.

We are indebted to Dr. Robert Rafford and the Middlebury Historical Society, for their kind assistance in our research and for supplying some of the illustrations used in this book; and to the Richard Seman family, present owners of the oldest house in Middlebury (1738) detailed in this book, for welcoming me into their home for photographs.

I am grateful for the cooperation and assistance of Charles C. Greene of the Princeton University Archives and to the folks at the Massachusetts Historical Society's Adams Papers Collection in the Electronic Archives.

Table of Contents

List of Illustrations

Old Route to Woodbury Map

Photo of Abbott's (formerly Bronson's) Pond

The Nathaniel Richardson Tavern in 1977

The Curtis-Wallace-Ruccio Homestead

The Original Breakneck School

A Mid-18th Century Map

Lieutenant Josiah Bronson

Brownstone Monuments of Bronson Children in Middlebury Cemetery

Human Remains Found at Breakneck—1959

Letter of John Adams to his wife Abigail, Jan. 17, 1777

Rochambeau Monument at Breakneck

General le Comte de Rochambeau

Rochambeau's Route to Breakneck from Barnes' Tavern, Southington

Rochambeau's Army Camp 9 at Breakneck

The Josiah Bronson House—1738

The Josiah Bronson House—2010

Photograph of the Door of the Poxe House at Breakneck

Two Views of the Inscriptions upon the Poxe House Door

Forward

"Unfortunately for us, the early Records of Waterbury have been, twice at least, harvested with an abundant portion of excellent historical grain left in the field, but no gleaners passing that way to garner it."
- Joseph Anderson D.D., 1896

No greater example of Dr. Anderson's discomfiture exists than the "historical grain" left in the verdant fields and granite hills of the little village called Breakneck, in the "The West Farms" of the Mattatuck Plantation. This delightful tract, in 1807, became incorporated as The Town of Middlebury, in central Connecticut. Records of the history of Middlebury are as scattered as the forgotten sheaves of wheat, which were left upon the threshing-room floor.

The earliest of those too oft forgotten "harvesters" was Dr. Henry Bronson, a direct descendant of the Bronsons of Breakneck, whose "History of Waterbury," was so eloquently written in 1858, just before the beginnings of the tragic and costly War Between the States. The scope of Dr. Bronson's work, in essence, described the evolution of Waterbury from its early beginnings as an outpost of Farmington to the close of the Revolutionary War. The work was completed within five years of Waterbury's Bicentennial celebration, just a half century after the independent Town of Middlebury came into being.

Charles W. Burpee compiled an extensive listing of men in service to the colony and later to our state, in his "Military History of Waterbury…" published in 1891. Many of the men included in this listing were from the West Farms and, more specifically, the area known as Breakneck. Just five years later, in 1896, the Rev. Joseph Anderson took up the pen and drew heavily upon Bronson's earlier writings, to create his monumental three-volume work, entitled "The Town and City of Waterbury, Connecticut, from the Aboriginal Period to the Year Eighteen Hundred and Ninety-five."

Middlebury had evolved from a section of the greater whole to a separate Church Society, and eventually to an independently incorporated Town. No section of town played a greater role in its evolution than that of Breakneck.

Writers and historians left the rolling hills and fertile fields of Middlebury untouched for nearly a century, until just a small passel of the remaining "historical grain" left in those fields, was at last gleaned, largely through the efforts of Miss Delia S. Bronson, beloved teacher, librarian and avid collector of Middlebury history. Although she bore his surname, she was not a descendant of the town's earliest settler, Isaac Bronson. Her nearly four volumes full of Middlebury facts were compiled into a Collective entitled: "History of Middlebury, Connecticut," and presented by the Middlebury Historical Society, Inc. in 1992. Regrettably, that work of the beloved Miss Bronson is just that: a collective of various stories, historical vignettes and facts, which leave the reader running from chapter to chapter, in order to gain some sense of continuity and historical order.

There were a few other "gleaners" along the way. Some, such as Katharine A. Prichard offered partial glimpses into Middlebury's past, in her "Ancient Burying-grounds of the Town of Waterbury, Connecticut...." of 1917, where she chronicled the deceased residents, who are laid to rest in the present Middlebury Cemetery. (Prichard also alludes to a much earlier cemetery within the bounds of present day Middlebury. But more on that later.) We owe her a debt of gratitude, in that many of the earliest grave markers are in such poor condition at present as to render them no longer readable. She has also compiled an earlier Work entitled: "Proprietors' Records of the Town of Waterbury, Connecticut 1677-1761," written in 1911, and chronicling just some of the land grants and events within the confines of the present town. The Mattatuck Historical Society published Miss Prichard's volumes.

Bradford E. Smith added "Middlebury, Connecticut Church and Vital Records, 1775 – 1900," in 1984. This work chronicles membership in the present Middlebury Congregational Church Society from its' inception. Dr. Robert A. Selig, in 1999, under the auspices of the Connecticut Historical Commission, produced a marvelous volume, documenting the march of the Comte de Rochambeau and his French army through Connecticut in 1781 and 1782. He provides a keen insight into the French army's visits to the "Breakneck" district of the present Middlebury, upon that army's march to and from the ultimate American victory at Yorktowne, Virginia.

But, in Dr. Anderson's words, "an abundant portion of excellent grain" still remains to be garnered, into the silos of Middlebury, for future generations to feast upon, and hopefully, with such grain, to become historically satiated.

This current volume is intended to offer some continuity to the earliest history of what is now Middlebury, in those tree-capped, rocky hills surrounding the great lake, which occupies much of its western quarter. We will attempt to glean just some of the remaining "grain" which was left behind, in the fields of the West Farms and the story-filled section of town called "Breakneck," in particular. This history too is far from complete, in so far as the original Proprietors' Records are rather incomplete. Then again, true history is never "complete."

One other significant reason for many deficiencies in the historical record of ancient Middlebury lies in the manner of describing locations, roads and early homesteads during the seventeenth and early eighteenth centuries, without reference to fixed positions. Descriptions of these early place names can be found in a separate Appendix to this book. In some cases, reference is made to long since lost landmarks such as piles of rocks or unusual trees. Nonetheless, this work is the author's humble attempt to provide his readers with as comprehensive a history of Middlebury's earliest settling as is feasibly possible and to treat the reader to just some of the more interesting and less well known stories of the little area known to locals and strangers alike, as Breakneck.

Chapter I

In the Beginnings...

The written history of the beautiful, little town of Middlebury begins, as do the histories of neighboring Waterbury and many other Connecticut towns, with the arrival of Englishmen to this region. There is no recorded evidence that native settlements ever existed in the vicinity of present-day Middlebury. Although this section of Waterbury was criss-crossed with ancient Native American trails, along which many of our early roads ran, the area no doubt accommodated, from time to time, a few small bands of natives along the banks of its numerous streams and along the shores of the great lake known to them as *Quassepaug*.

In 1981, archaeological excavations on farm property near the corner of Watertown Road and Breakneck Hill Road, owned at the time by Leroy Foote, revealed a Native American camp site (site 81-001) from the Late Archaic Period. (6,000 to 3,700 years ago) Discovered along the banks of a branch of the Hop Brook were a number of small-stem quartz points, small triangular projectile points (arrowheads), quartz knives and so-called side-notched Brewerton points. [1]

In 1988, an archaeological survey of the Hop Brook Dam area (site 88-008) from the Terminal Archaic Period (3,700 to 2,700 years ago) disclosed a wealth of Native American artifacts including projectile points, stone knives and other bi-faced tools, scrapers, retouched stone flakes and debris from creating these artifacts. The site was actually radio-carbon dated to 3,470 years ago. [2]

1   See WAL Summary. Report of the Middlebury Golf Community
2   Ibid.

Connecticut archaeologists, in the spring of 2004, explored five areas of the new condominium complex called Ridgewood, and its planned golf community off Route 188. The parcel consisted of some three hundred acres. Reportedly, at least four "living floors" with hearths, two fire pits and an accumulation of artifacts including arrowheads were discovered along the confluence of two streams, which course through the property. Good charcoal samples from one site referred to as A-South, could be Carbon dated to the Late to Terminal Archaic Periods, some 5,000 to 3,000 years ago.[3]

But all of these artifacts were left behind by a migratory people; perhaps some of the Pootatucks from the area which is now Southbury. The closest Native American settlement to the present Middlebury lay in that town, then called "Pomperaug" and so named for the chief of the Pootatucks, a sub-tribe of the Derby Indians or Paugussucks It was from this tribe that the land composing present-day Woodbury was purchased.

Most of the land presently encompassing the town of Middlebury was once a part of the original Mattatuck Plantation. In the mid 17th Century, local tribes ceded it to residents of Farmington, through at least four ancient deeds. The original owners of this land were members of the Algonkian-speaking tribes and, no doubt, included the Tunxis tribe to the north and east, and the aforementioned Paugussucks to the south and west.

These were quite friendly peoples amongst themselves and, in all probability, may have likely inter-married. Those earliest deeds, given the many overlapping signatures, indicated some degree of interrelationship between the two tribes. It is curious that the land encompassing the West Farms, as Middlebury was first known to the earliest settlers seems to have been included in deeds signed both by the Tunxis and by the Paugussuck tribes. And although but a few Native American names exist upon those original Deeds, their tribal numbers and general ethnological condition are unknown.

The earliest Deed of February 8, 1657,[4] held in the land records of Farmington, indicated a "parcel or tract of land called Matetacoke" conveyed to William Lewis and Samuel Steele of that town. The native name for this area could literally be translated as a: "place without trees." That first deed was signed with the marks of local natives including Kepaquamp, Querrimus and Mataneage, all members of the Tunxis, or Farmington,

3   Ibid.
4   BRH, p. 2-3.

Indian Tribe, whose primary camp-grounds lay in that town. Petthuzzo and Toxerunnck, successors of these earliest of local native chiefs, signed a much later deed in follow-up to the above, dated August 11, 1718. [5]

On August 26, 1674, the first deed to actually reference the establishment of a plantation at Mattatuck, a tract of land lying on both sides of the "Mattatuck" River, "measuring some ten miles from north to south, and six miles in breadth," was conveyed to the original proprietors. Some 85,000 acres stretched from Farmington to the north and as far as Derby to the south. The land included Cheshire to the east and extended to Woodbury in the west. This deed bears the marks of some fourteen natives. Recurring names in the Tunxis Deeds include John a Compowne, [6]Mantow,[7]Atumtucko and Spinning Squaw. [8] It is of interest that a woman made her mark upon that deed.

Nearly ten years later, on April 29, 1684, Patucko, on behalf of the aforesaid Atumtucko and the others, signed another deed, relating more to the purchase of the northern section of the plantation. [9]

A third deed in this series, given by the Tunxis Indians, was dated December 2, 1684 and also included Atumtucko, while the names of Spinning Squaw, John a Compowne and Manitow reappear. In this series of three deeds given by the Farmington Indians, a total of twenty-five names appear. This group represented a total population of about four hundred.

One further deed, dated February 20, 1685, [10] and held in the Waterbury Land Records, Vol. II, pp. 224-231,was given by the Paugasuck, or Derby Indians, conveying parcels included in the 1657 Deed, a curious anomaly. Were it not strange enough that the deeded lands overlapped, but four of the original grantors were women. They were most likely widowed squaws. Anderson is unsure of the relationship between the two tribes but suggests, perhaps, that the signers were inter-related through marriage. The Paugasuck (possibly a misspelling of "Paugussuck") [11] tribe's

---

5   Ibid. p. 3.
6   Lake Compounce in Bristol takes its name from this Chief
7   Mount Tobe in Plymouth takes its name from this Chief
8   AND, p. 28.
9   Ibid. p. 30.
10   Ibid.
11   Today this tribe is known as the Paugussets, but are not recognized currently as a "tribe" and numerous claims to lands in Southbury and surrounds have been overturned.

main campground, actually a makeshift fortress, lay further south at the juncture of the Naugatuck and Housatonic Rivers. This deed conveyed some twenty parcels of land to the Mattatuck settlers. The 1684 deed set the western boundary at "Cedar Swamp, the Middle of Toamtick [12] Pond, (Long Meadow Pond) Quasepaug Pond and Woodbury bounds." Henry Bronson refers to a point "four score rods [13] from the easternmost point of Quasepaug Pond, on the Woodbury Road." [14] Parcels of conveyed lands on the west side of the river were given "place names" in that deed including Saracasks, Petowtucke, Weqarunsh, Capage, Cocumpasucke, Mequenhuttocke, Panootan, Mattuckhott, cocacocks, Quarasksucks, Towantucke and half of the "Cedar Swamp." [15] Towantucke is readily recognizable but other of these "place names" may have also lain in the bounds of present-day Middlebury.

A series of long ridges or "hills," branded with various names over the years, make up much of the present town. These tend to separate broad meadows, often boggy, and provide watersheds for the many streams, which course through them. Most prominent among these are the two branches of Hop Brook located in Breakneck, the Goat Brook entering Hop Brook from the west, Long Meadow Brook and Eight Mile Brook, forming the western bounds of the present town. The large lake, mentioned in the Paugasuck deed, which was known, then as now, as "Quassapaug", occupies the northwestern reaches of the town.

A number of interpretations of the name have been offered over the years, each deriving from the Algonkin language. William Cothren, in his "History of Woodbury," attributed the meaning: "the Beautiful Clear Water," to Captain John Miner. [16] Cothren, himself, suggests "rocky pond," from the native root *qussuk* meaning "rock" or "stone." The origin of "paug" is taken from the Algonkin *pe-auke,* referring to standing water, as opposed to a river or stream. Dr. Anderson suggests that the name might represent *quunnosu-paug,* or "pickerel pond," while Dr. James Hammond Trumbull, former state librarian and Secretary of the State, in his "Indian Names of Places in Connecticut" of 1881, suggests *k'che-paug,* or "greatest pond,"

---

12 This name is still in use today as "Toantic."

13 About one quarter mile.

14 BRH, p. 63.

15 AND, p. 39.

16 Miner was born in Charlestown, Massachusetts in 1635, a first generation New Englander. He was a founder of Stratford, Connecticut before moving to Woodbury, where he died in 1719.

which, in the author's opinion, seems most likely to be correct. In a report concerning boundaries, made by agents of Woodbury and Mattatuck, dated June 29, 1680, the lake is referred to as "the great pond." Given the fact that the present Lake Candlewood is man-made, the lake now called Quassapaug was the largest natural lake in western Connecticut. The natives would have been well aware of this fact. It is drained by what was once known as Quassapaug River, now Eight Mile Brook, which eventually empties into the Housatonic.

Small portions of the present town were also included in the original lands of Southbury and Woodbury. In a Woodbury Deed, dated October 30, 1687, this pond is mentioned as "the pond called and commonly known by the name Quassapaug." The eastern boundary of that town was said to be "four score rod (actually 87 rods) eastward of the easternmost of the pond." The original eastern bounds of Woodbury roughly correspond to Tranquility and old Watertown Roads.

Mentioned in at least two of the original Deeds is the place called *Towantucke,* (Towantic) perhaps the only additional name presently recognizable out of the original twenty parcels conveyed to the early planters. As aforesaid, this no doubt refers to the area presently occupied by Long Meadow Pond and clearly indicates that the original "Mattatuck" purchase encompassed what was once known as the Gunntown section of present-day Middlebury. So too, the "Cedar Swamp" north of Lake Quassapaug is mentioned in the original deed, as noted above, but no local name is ascribed to it. To identify any of the other "twenty parcels," Anderson points out is "quite impossible." [17]

Anderson describes physical evidence of the earliest peoples who may have transiently lived here. Stone implements were discovered in the Bradleyville section (the area of Hop Brook dam just north of present Naugatuck) by John Bradley, Isaac Scott and Enoch Newton, many years ago.[18] Bradley had a knife factory in this area. Very few reports of such physical evidence have surfaced since.

Rumor has it that on the plain east of Three Mile Hill, near to where the Memorial Middle School is situated at present, Native Americans of the region gathered for their annual games; sort of a Native American Olympics, which included foot races. Hence, the area was once known as "Race Plain." [19] This area was also known as "Bronson's Meadow"

---

17   AND, p. 40.
18   Ibid. p. 61.
19   Ibid. p. 707.

and, at a later date, accommodated the Kelly and Robins' farms. The old Nathaniel Richardson homestead, one of the area's earliest, lay on the southern end of this meadow, on the Woodbury (Kelly) road. Richardson reportedly kept a tavern there. The house was unfortunately torn down in the nineteen seventies for reasons of safety, as it gradually fell into disrepair. Dr. Anderson suggests that General George Washington stopped there. It was rumored that Rochambeau may have stayed there as well, but this too is highly unlikely. In all probability, it was a later Nathaniel Richardson, whose house is located further up the hill at the corner of Acme Drive, who entertained General Washington. One of the earliest homesteads in Breakneck, the earlier Nathaniel Richardson place will be described more fully in a subsequent chapter. Its stone cellar remains. The foundation and hand-dug, stone-lined well of the Robins' place, formerly the home of Ebenezer Richardson, Nathaniel II's father, is also still visible (2010) on the south side of Kelly Road, a short distance to the west, as one begins the ascent up Three Mile Hill from Memorial Drive.

Chapter II

Planting the Seeds...

By October of 1644, there existed six towns in the Colony of Connecticut. They included Hartford, Windsor, Wethersfield, Stratford, Uncoa or Fairfield; and Southampton, on the Long Island. [20] In addition to these settlements, John Winthrop Jr. had already established the Colony of Saybrooke in 1636, named after Viscount Saye & Sele and Lord Brooke, the prime financial backers of the endeavor, at the mouth of the Connecticut River. The Colony of New Haven was established in 1638, under the leadership of Rev. John Davenport, a persecuted puritan minister from London, together with Theophilus Eaton of the Massachusetts Bay Colony.

While settlers established outposts at Windsor and Wethersfield a year or two earlier, the Rev. Thomas Hooker led a group of about sixty settlers from Newtowne, [21] in the Colony of Massachusetts Bay, to establish a new settlement in 1636, on the banks of the Connecticut River at Suckiag, today known as Hartford. With the continued populating of Hartford over the next several years and the ever-present need for new lands, the General Court of the newly formed Connecticut Colony began exploring the feasibility of establishing new towns in the area.

On December 1st of 1645, Farmington was set out as the plantation of Tunxis, subsequently given its English name and its bounds established. Other plantations soon followed. By 1672 (or 1673, under the Julian calendar) over eighty men and their families inhabited the place. Dr. Anderson concluded:

---

20 Ibid. p. 105.
21 Today known as Cambridge, Massachusetts

"It will never be possible for any investigator to determine what Englishman first beheld the lands on which we dwell in Waterbury (including the lands of present-day Middlebury) or to declare the purpose that led him into the valley through which ran the Mattatuck River." [22]

We do know that in 1657, two men of "Farmingtowne" in the person of John Standley and John Andrews, who later joined to the original planters, set out for the area in search of metals, particularly lead, for the making of ammunition. They returned from their explorations, with a substance they called "black lead." It turned out not to be related to the prized element at all. [23]

However, the discovery still inspired interest in the valley of the Mattatuck and, by the year 1673, twenty-six men of Farmington, through their representative John Lankton, sent up a petition to the General Court of the Connecticut Colony, for a plantation at Mattatuck:

THE PETITION FOR A PLANTATION [24]

"To the honerd generall court now sitting in Hartford October 9, 73"

"Honerd gentlemen and fathers we being sensible of our great neede of a comfortable subsistence doe hereby make our address to your selves In order to the same Not Questioning your ceare and faithfulness In Ye premisses; allso hoping of your freeness and readyness to accomidate your poore supplicants with Yt which we Judge to be: In your hands: according to an orderly proseeding we therefore whose names are hereafter Inserted to humbly petition your honours to take cognicance: of our state who want Land to Labour upon: for our subsistance & now having found out a trackt at a place called by ye Indians matitacoock: which we aprihend may sufetiently acomidate to make a small plantation: we are therefore bound hereby to petition your honours to grant vs ye liberty of planting ye same with as many others as may be: capable comfortably to entertaine and as for the purchasing of ye natives with your alowance we shall take care of: & so not to trouble with farther Inlargement we rest only desiring your due consideration & a return By our Louing ffriend John Lankton and subscribe our selfes your nedy petitioners"

---

22 AND, p. 116.
23 Ibid. p. 117.
24 Ibid. p. 123.

Signatories:
Thomas Newell , Daniell warner

John Lankton	**Abraham Andrews**
John andrews	*Thomas hancox*
John warner senio'r	*John Carrington*
Daniell porter	*Daniell Andrews*
Edmun Scoot	*Joseph heacox*
John Standly Junior	*thomas standly*
abraham brounsen	**Obadiah Richards** [25]
Richard seamer	*Timothy standley*
John Warner Junio'r	*william higgeson*
Isack brounsen	*John porter*
Samuell heacox	*Thomas Barnes*
John Wellton	*John woodruff*

A few surnames from that petition figure prominently in the history of Middlebury, to wit: brounsen (Bronson), Porter and Warner.

The answer from the General Court was received on October 9, 1673.

THE ANSWER OF THE COURT TO THE PETITION FOR A PLANTATION [26]

Oct. 9, 1673

"*In answer to the petition of severall inhabitants of the town of Farmington that Mattatock that those lands might be granted for a plantation, this Court have seen cause to order that those lands may be viewed sometime between this and the Court of May next, and that reporte be made to the Court in May next, whether it be judged fitt to make a plantation. The Committee appoynted are L'wt Tho: Bull, L'wt Rob't Webster and Daniel Pratt.*"

The committee thus appointed, returned its findings of a site visit over four successive days in early April 1674. Nicholas Olmstead was substituted for Daniel Pratt, for an undisclosed reason.

---

25 This signature appears to be in a different hand-writing style.
26 AND, p. 124.

THE COMMITTEE REPORT TO THE COURT
CONCERNING MATTATOCK [27]

April 6, 7, 8, 9, 1674

"Wee, whos names are underwritten (according to the desire and appointment of ye honoured Court) have viewed ye lands upon Mattatuck river in order to a plantation, we doe apprehend that there is about six hundred acres of meadow and plowing land lying on both sides of ye river besides upland convenient for a towne plot, with a suitable out let into ye woods on ye west of ye river, and good feeding land for cattell.

The meadow & plowing land above written a considerable part of it lyeth in two pieces near ye town plot, ye rest in smaller parcels, ye farthest of which we judge not above fower miles from ye town plot: and our apprehensions are that it may accommodate thirty families"

Thomas Bull
Nicho: Olmstead
Robert Webster

The "two pieces" referred to above are, according to Henry Bronson, the level river lands on the east side of the river, called Manhan or Mahan Meadow; and the west side of the River near the mouth of Steel's Brook. [28] The "farthest" lands were, in all likelihood, Judd's Meadow, present-day Naugatuck - or adjacent Oxford. It may well be that Bull, Olmstead and Webster set foot within the bounds of present-day Middlebury, in that the "Return" indicates a "suitable out let into ye woods on ye west of ye river...." This sentence, Anderson suggests, may have referred to Mattatuck's access to Woodbury. (perhaps along the ancient Indian trail!) The latter town had been recently platted by four men from the Derby plantation, who had been directed "to erect a plantation at Pomperoage." Fifteen dissident members of Rev. Zecheriah Walker's congregation and their families arrived there in 1772/3 from what is now Stratford.

On the 19th day of May, 1673/4, the General Court, after receiving the exploratory report, appointed Maj. John Talcott, Lt. Robert Webster, Lt. Nicholas Olmstead, Ens. Samuel Steele and Ens. John Wadsworth to *"regulate and order the seteling of a plantation at Mattatock in the most*

27 Ibid.
28 Present-day Watertown.

suitable way that may be." [29] Thus, Waterbury, and hence Middlebury, was officially created.

The Committee established the Laws and Covenants of the plantation, which was to become the twenty-sixth town within the bounds of the Connecticut Colony. Anderson elucidates the formula of obligations and agreements, which covered eight basic conditions for establishing said plantation. [30] These Articles obviously applied to the area known as West Farms, as well.

The first of these Articles permitted every "acceptable" inhabitant to have eight acres for a house lot. The second provided for the amount of land distributed to each planter in the "meadows," to be based upon each man's estate, but limited to one hundred Pounds. This Article no doubt formed the basis for doling out lands in West Farms.

Thirdly, the payment of public charges, for a period of five years, was to be covered by a tax upon the meadows. The fourth provision required that every man take up allotments within four years of the date of "the Articles," be required to build *a "good, substantial dwelling house, at least eighteen feet long, sixteen feet wide, and nine feet between joists, and with a good chimney."*

The fifth Article reinforced the previous one, in requiring compliance in every particular. Sixth, each allottee, having built his house, was required to take up residence in it within four specified years. This Article and the next provided some confusion in researching the provenance of early Middlebury houses.

The seventh provision required a man who has built his house to live in it for four years, before coming into full ownership. Lastly, every allottee was required to subscribe to the "Articles" by his signature or by his mark.

To the original "Articles," thirty-nine names were appended. Later names were added bringing the total number of original Planters to forty-two. History failed to record how many men actually accepted house lots, nor do we know how many inhabitants existed in the years of 1674 and 1675, at the "old towne plott," located high upon the protection of West Side Hill, in the vicinity of the present Chase Park. Reference was actually made to "the new towne going up at Mattatuck" in documents of the General Court of Connecticut Colony in May of 1675. [31]

---

29 AND, p. 126.
30 Ibid. p. 127.
31 Ibid. p. 134.

Soon thereafter, a dark pall cast a long shadow upon the infant plantation. Miantonomah (Metacomet), better known as "King Philip," and grandson of the great Massasoit of the Wampanouags, began his attacks upon white settlers in eastern Connecticut, wherever and whenever feasible. This uprising was known as "The Great Indian War of New England" or, more simply, as "King Philip's War." On October 14, 1675, the General Court ordered that all indefensible plantations, including that of Mattatuck, withdraw to the protection of the towns. [32] Only the town of Simsbury, in Connecticut, was actually destroyed during the uprising but all of the settlers had already returned safely to Hartford.

Thus it was that the initial Planters abandoned the original settlement at "towne plott," and returned to Farmington. Men of Woodbury (Pomperauge) returned to Stratford, from whence they came, and resettled only reluctantly when "King Philip's War" was at last over and it was safe to return. [33] In contrast, the proprietors of the abandoned plantation at Mattatuck were more than anxious to return.

But the court had issued an edict that all future plantations or townships *"shall settle themselves in such nearness together that they may be a help, defense and succor each to other against any surprise, onset or attempt of any common enemie."*[34] Further, at a meeting in Farmington, held in May of 1677, the proprietors had raised the question of an unidentified "difficulty," which they had encountered in laying out the original town plot.

Thus, it came to pass that, upon recommendation of a "Grand committee," a new site was chosen to the east of "the Great River," near the center of the present City of Waterbury. This consisted of smaller house lots, proximity to numerous water sources and a place for a corn mill, upon the "Roaring River." (the Mad River) Because of the numerous streams and rivulets, which coursed through the new site, effectively dividing it into several "islands," the name of the new plantation was given as "Watterbury."

Over the course of the years from 1677 to 1682, a number of meetings of the "Grand committee" of Mattatuck were called. During this period, as well, houses were constructed and habitation ensued. It was at the meeting in January, 1677 that the committee appointed men, including Benjamin Judd, resident surveyor, and Lieutenant Samuel Steele "to lay out all necessary highways for the use of the inhabitants that were

32   Ibid. p. 137.
33   Ibid.
34   Ibid. p. 145.

needful." [35] In all probability, one of these "needful" highways followed the old Waterbury-Woodbury Road up Waterbury's West Side Hill and on through present-day Middlebury, crossing over Breakneck Hill, passing "north of the pond,"[Quassapaug] and on into the evolving plantation at Woodbury, along what is today White Deer Rocks Road. In June of 1720, Isaac Bronson, Timothy Standly and Thomas Judd were formally charged with laying out a "rode towards Woodbury," commencing at "the weste bars, (the left bank of the Naugatuck River) "being twenty rods wide for a distance up the hill, running by Isaac Bronson's farm" (at Breakneck) and "ending at the going down of Wolfpit Hill to the Bridg (Bride's) Brook at Woodbury bounds." [36]

The early planners laid out house lots of approximately two to four acres, in cross-like fashion at Waterbury's present Exchange Place, with highways running in the direction of the four points of the compass. Anderson notes that: "uplands were permitted to be added to the meadow lands of Isaac Bronson" while planters Daniel Porter and Thomas Richardson had applied for, and were granted additional lands. There is some evidence to suggest that at least some of these lands were in the West Farms. Thomas Richardson is of particular note, for it was his daughter Rebecca, born to his Goodwife Mary, on April 27, 1679, who was the first English child born at Mattatuck.

At a meeting in Hartford on May 22, 1680, a committee consisting of William Judd, Thomas Judd, John Standley and "such others as the inhabitants of Mattatuck shall appoint" to meet with Woodbury for the purpose of establishing a "bound line" between the two towns. This would be the precursor line dividing the towns of Middlebury and Woodbury of today. [37] The Proprietors' Records of May 31, 1680 indicate that a committee of two was appointed to meet with "Or Hon'd ffriends of woodbery" to set the bounds between that village and Mattatuck. The two were John Welton and Samuel Hickox. They no doubt may have travelled over the rough road now known as Breakneck Hill. On June 29, 1680, these men, together with John Minor, Joseph Judson and Israel Curtice, representing Woodbury, agreed upon the western boundary of *Mattatuck.* Cothren, in his "History of Ancient Woodbury," tells us that in the third purchase of land from the Pootatucks of that area, the eastern bounds of that village

35   Ibid. 151.
36   This road follows what is now White Deer Rocks Road into Woodbury.
37   AND, p. 155.

were set at "Four score rod eastward of ye Easternmost of ye pond Called and commonly known by ye Name Quassapaug." [38]

It would be best, at this point, to employ Rev. Anderson's description of the route one would take, in those early days, in travelling from what is now Waterbury on into Woodbury. [39] He writes:

In going from Waterbury to Middlebury the first ascent is upon the West Side hill, first so named in a grant made to Samuel Barnes between 1730 and 1733. Next to the right is Bryant's hill. Pass Tamarack swamp and Richards' hill is at your right as you are passing through the swamp. Pass the Boughton place and Arnold's hill lies to your left. Cross the Peat swamp and at your right lies Gaylord's hill. Lemuel Nichols' tavern before the revolution – now [1896] an old house stands on this hill. A quarter of a mile further on, and Oronoke hill is on your left. The Umberfield place is on the north end of this hill. (a small road opposite Woodside Road and the transfer station would have led to this homestead and is presently known as Umberfield's Road) *The John Hine place was in the vicinity. Cross Gaylord's brook, and to your right is Two-and-a-half Mile hill – the southern end of which hill is the rock known as Pine rock – a boundary point between Waterbury and Middlebury.* [40]

The reader should recall that the old Middlebury road swept around this rock, to the south and the "rock cut" off Exit 17 of I-84, through this hill, did not exist at that time. Anderson continues: *The western slope of the above hill is now known as Mount Fair. Between the Two-and-a-half Mile hill and the Three-mile hill, you pass Bissell's hill on the left, which still bears that name. The old Morse [Moss] road went over this hill, and on it were several houses, and later a blacksmith shop belonging to Joseph Peck. Three Mile hill was named, I know not how early, but it is mentioned in 1720.* The road continued over Break Neck hill, to White Deer Rocks road to the north of the lake and on into Woodbury *at the going down of Wolf Pit hill to the Brid[e]'s brook in Woodbury bounds.* From the Straits Turnpike at Route 64, the old Woodbury road coursed up Kelly Road to Colonial Drive and onto Breakneck Hill Road, where, beginning with Isaac Brounsen [Bronson] the Planter, before 1702, the earliest settlers of present-day Middlebury built their homes.

---

38 WMC, p. 26.
39 Ibid. p. 354
40 Ibid.

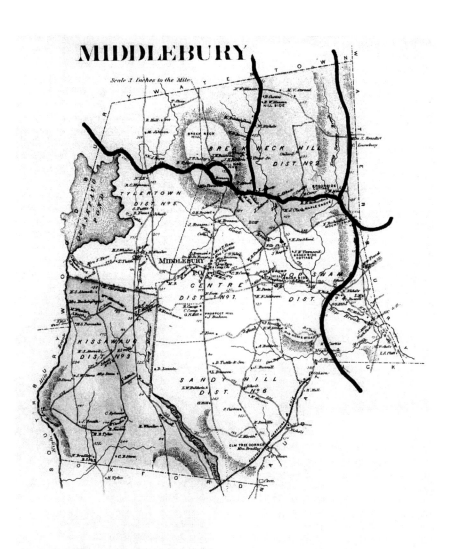

Fig. 1 – Ancient Route from Waterbury to Woodbury circa 1702

From the junction of Routes 63 and 64, Anderson also takes one over a later route along the current Middlebury road to Tucker Hill road towards the present Green and he describes this road thus: *When you have reached Middlebury-Four-Corners, you have passed the southern end of this hill.* [Three Mile Hill] *The village of Middlebury is upon the northern end of the ridge to which the name of Bedlam was applied very early. Beyond Middlebury, and next Lake Quassapaug, lies the hill known in 1686 as the Great Hill east of Quassapaug.* [41] This route continued, at the western shore of the lake, onto the Old Waterbury road and Old Ben Sherman Hill to Woodbury. Thus, by the 1800s, there were two major routes to that village from what is now Waterbury.

By 1681, Mattatuck was a village of twenty-eight dwelling houses, occupied by 145 "legalized souls." That number excludes those individuals who were indentured to settlers and "Indians," as well. Four of these "legalized souls" were the children of Isaac Bronson. They included Isaac, jr., age 11 years; John, age 8 years; Samuel, age 5 years; and Mary, age 1 year: all born in Farmington. Four more of these "legalized souls" included the children of Isaac's brother, John: John, age 11; Sarah, age 9; Dorothy, age 6; and Ebenezer, age 4.

At the meeting of Proprietors held on April 17, 1688, the first reference to Breakneck is offered. For, at that meeting, the following grants of land were approved: *"thomas worner to have too acers for on in ye divition of meadow at ye southward end of ye breakneck hill as we go to woodbury and so to take up his whol divition.* [Perhaps in the area of Fenn's farm] *To john brunson was granted to take up his divition in ye same measur joind to his bogey meadow.* (This would suggest an earlier grant to John of his "boggy meadow." *to isaac brunson was granted his divition on ye east side Race Playn buting north on ye high way to woodbury to spring south to have too acers for one as others above said…"* [42](this area would be close to the present Memorial Middle School). The records of a Town Meeting held on December 30, 1687 also reveal that the members of Mattatuck Plantation had *"granted to George Scott six acres of boggy meadow or moving land on the north branch of Hop Brook where the brooks meet and to run up the south branch."* [43] These were apparently the first recorded land grants specifically referenced as in the West Farms and, hence, within the present

41 Ibid.
42 KAP, p. 225-26.
43 Ibid. p. 215.

town of Middlebury. Other grants would follow. On May 15, 1699, for example, the Proprietors *"granted Benjamin Barnes ten acres of upland at breakneck hill adjoining to the Warners."*[44] Anderson tells us that until 1700, Mattatuck was a "Compact village." Only after this time did individuals begin moving away from the town centre.

It was, in all likelihood, Isaac, the planter, [srg Brunson] who constructed the first-known dwelling house in the Breakneck section of the West Farms, some time before April 6, of 1702. [45] The presence of this house is documented in the Proprietors' Records of that date, to wit: *"att ye same meeting srg brunson had teen acers of upland given him at breakneck hill joyning to his own land.* [A reference perhaps to the above grant of 1688] *At ye same meeting there was granted to srg brunson for acers and a half and joseph gaylard senor for acers and a half where brunsons house stands at breakneck hill."*[46]

In June of the prior year of 1701, Bronson had already purchased of Thomas Warner, the twelve acres on the north side of the Woodbury Road, assumedly including the grant of acreage in 1688, as noted above. [47] There is no evidence that Warner ever built on his land at Breakneck.

Another grant of land in the West Farms would occur at the meeting of January 7, 1705: "there was *granted to Stephen upson seven or eyght acers of bogey meadow south west of hop brook not pregedising former grants."*[48]

On December 23, 1700, Isaac Jr. had also been accepted as a Proprietor inhabitant. [49] We cannot find a record of Isaac's brother John becoming one but those records, as reprinted by Katherine Prichard, are incomplete.

However, at the Proprietors' meeting of April 9, 1705, land was granted, on the south side of Breakneck Hill Road, to both of the planter's sons: Isaac Jr. and John. *"At ye same meeting ye proprietors gave isaac brunson jur and john brunson twelve acers of land on ye south sd woodbury Road joyning to breakneck hill provided they build on it."* Further records seem to indicate that both of the Bronson brothers built houses in Breakneck. Isaac Jr.'s house was likely located where the James C. Tyler house stands, just west of Tyler Crossing.

---

44 Ibid. p. 50.
45 AND, p. 252.
46 KAP. P. 55.
47 BRH, p. 41. See note.
48 KAP, p. 66.
49 Ibid.

In 1716, Isaac Bronson, the Planter, quitclaimed his rights to his north side property to his son Isaac Jr. It is generally believed, according to a tradition in the family that, in that house of his son, the first English child of West Farms, Isaac III, was born March 27, 1707. [50] This house on Breakneck Hill road was torn down and replaced with the Tyler house. Isaac Jr. built the first sawmill on Hop Brook, creating what is presently known as "Abbott's" Pond, to provide the waterpower to run it. We will see later that the French visitors of Rochambeau's army were very impressed with the mill's output.

Abbott's Pond at Breakneck – created by Isaac Bronson in 1702 to support his saw mill on Hop Brook (R. Sullivan photo)

Other lands had also been granted in the Breakneck area early on. At a Proprietors' Meeting of February 19, 1707 – 08, they *"granted ebenezer worner to take his part in ye divition above agreed on acording to his interest in his fathers lot in ye bogey meadow yt lys north west of serg brunsons meadow westward of break neck hill."* [51] At the Proprietors' meeting on the *"first Monday in February, 1751,"* Breakneck is yet again mentioned. In this

---

50   Ibid.
51   Ibid. p. 75.

instance, "*Dr. Ebenezer Worner of Woodbury lay out for acres and a quarter of land In the undivided land in said Waterbury In Lew of eleven acres and a quarter of boggy meadow in a meadow west of Break Neck Hill that he had liberty to take as his part of a division Granted on his father's propriety...*" [52] This property lay west of Breakneck in what would later be called the Tylertown district and extended to what is now Tranquility Road as it continues onto Old Watertown Road. Again, at one time this highway formed the western boundary of Waterbury with Woodbury.

Isaac Bronson III received a deed of ownership in 1734, from his father before him, by virtue of being the eldest child. It consisted of, in addition to the house and glass contained therein, some four acres of land. [53] Isaac III did have an older sister named Jerusha, who was born November 8th, 1703 and later married Paul Welch. She was, in all likelihood, born in Waterbury town. However, it is indeed possible that she was the first child born within the present Middlebury boundaries, despite the fact that her brother Isaac's tombstone in the present cemetery and long-standing family tradition indicate that he was the first.

John Brounsen, (Bronson) the second son of Isaac the Planter, was, as noted above, supposed to have lived at Breakneck also. John had a house of his own there, and twenty-two acres of land, February 27, 1705-6, which he bought by exchange with Joseph Gaylord Sr. [54] It is not clear whether Gaylord ever lived in Breakneck before this time, although it is quite plausible. John later built a house on the present Cherry Street in Waterbury.

Lieutenant Josiah Bronson, brother of Isaac II, built a house a little north from the "Irving Baldwin house," [55] (located near the corner of Breakneck Hill and Artillery Roads) which was built circa 1750. Lieut. Josiah's house still stands, as the oldest house in present-day Middlebury (1738) and was formerly owned by the late Middlebury historian, Laurence Duryea, who meticulously restored it. The Richard Seman family now owns the house.

James Bronson, born in 1727 and brother to Isaac Jr. and Josiah, built a home on the south end of Breakneck Hill, in the area of where Artillery Road meets Charcoal Avenue about 1760. This was about ten years after

52 KAP. P. 75.
53 BRD, p. 8.
54 BRH, p. 146.
55 BRD, p. 4.

he married Sarah Brocket of Wallingford. "This house lay on land formerly owned by Thomas Warner, as granted in 1688." [56]

Delia Bronson also records that Stephen Abbott came from Branford about 1750 and settled at Breakneck, perhaps on the north side of the road, near Tyler Crossing. His grandson, David, married Sarah Tyler, daughter of the above- mentioned James C. Tyler, in 1786 and may have built the house on the corner of Breakneck Hill and Watertown Roads, where the late Mr. and Mrs. Leroy Foote lived. [57] Later descendants of the Abbotts lived in the area of what is now known as Abbott's Pond for many years.

As was already mentioned, Isaac Bronson Jr. originally created this pond some time after 1700, to supply the area's first sawmill with power. Isaac Bronson III was granted permission at a Town Meeting held in Waterbury in 1784, to rebuild the mill and dam at that pond, provided he maintain the bridge over it. [58] One can only wonder what kind of shape that little bridge was in when several thousand men, a baggage train and several artillery caissons of Rochambeau's army rumbled over it, three years before it was reconstructed.

The Richardson (Richason) family of Mattatuck, was also granted property in the area of Breakneck. Nathaniel Richardson, about 24 years in age, born on May 28, 1686 to Thomas Richardson, the Planter, and his wife, Mary, was one of four men from Waterbury, sent to Canada in May of 1709, to fight the French, in what was commonly known as "Queen Anne's War." He would hold the distinction of being the first soldier in any war of the colonies to settle in what is now Middlebury.

In October of 1709, Queen Anne (recall that Connecticut was still an English Colony) ordered the Canadian expedition to be "laid aside." After a bout of illness while in New Haven, Nathaniel returned to Waterbury and was granted *"four*-score *acres on a branch of the Hop Brook east from Breakneck Hill"* on March 13, 1710 - 11. Until a few years ago, as aforementioned, the house still stood on Kelly Road, north of Memorial School. As has been the case with many early landmarks, this house proved to be a decrepit though rather attractive nuisance, lending itself an easy mark for the curiosity of children. Regrettably, its historical significance was insufficient to save it from the wrecker's ball. Rumor had it that it too served as a tavern during the Revolutionary period.

---

56   Ibid.
57   Ibid. p. 5.
58   Ibid. p. 135.

The Proprietors' Records of the settlement at Waterbury, dated March 13, 1710 contain this land grant, " *by a mager vott give nathanill richason for scor acurs of land in the north sid the rood to Woodbury up the grat brok est from break neck hill to be taken in good forme in one peis…*"and with the customary stipulations: *"one this condition that he tak it as his hole proprity as a bachelder's accomydation and cohabit ten yers in the town in a settled wa [y] s and bild a tenetabel hous acording to originell articels.….*" [59]

Nathaniel Richardson Tavern razed in 1977
(Middlebury Historical Society collection)

This property was located west of two and one half mile hill and also west of what was then called the "Moses [Moss] road." As was said previously, this road likely ran from the Salem society (present-day Naugatuck) onto the Woodbury road, just opposite Memorial School, to what is now Straits Turnpike. One can still make out a portion of the old roadbed behind the plot where the Kelly homestead stood, alongside Richardson's "tavern." Straits Turnpike was not laid out in the area until 1760.

---

59   KAP, p. 80.

Nathaniel died on November 3, 1712 – 13, from the "great sickness" [60] as did his parents, Thomas Sr. and Mary Richardson and two brothers, having already secured the rights to his property. That property subsequently went to his remaining brothers and sisters. Nathaniel's brother Ebenezer, *"a man who loved the Wilderness,"* according to Anderson, *"and moved into it anew whenever neighbors came into view – went at last to live at Breakneck."* The cellar and well of Ebinezer's home can still be seen just above the Memorial Middle School on the south side of what is now Kelly Road (the Woodbury Road). He, together with his wife, Margit Warner, had six children there.

"Margit," (probably Margaret) daughter of Thomas Warner, died in June of 1749 and Ebinezer remarried, just four months later, to Hannah, the widow of John Bronson. A personal communication of the author corroborates the fact that Ebinezer's son, Thomas, inherited from his father *"twenty acres of Land upon the east side of three mile hill which is the Land I had of Joseph Nichols also Eight acres of Land at the South end of three mile hill buting North and West on Thompson and Judsons Land on Capt. Nichols and East on my own land."* This lay west of Ebinezer's property. High on the hill to the west, Thomas likely built his own home about 1760, the Curtiss - Wallace house. Francis and Lydia Ruccio restored the house, in the 1970s. It is still standing, altered somewhat, from the original by its more modern additions, on the corner of Kelly Road at its junction with Acme Drive, this latter road not laid out until the 20th Century.

The Richardsons raised eight children in the little frame house, which faced east to the morning sun, on the north side of the Woodbury road. [61] Their daughter, Tamer, who was born on the 13th day of September 1758 and her link to the Revolution, will be covered in a subsequent chapter. From all of the above, it seems quite clear that the main "center" of development in West Farms would be along the route to Woodbury, called Breakneck.

---

60   This most likely was Smallpox.
61   This includes the present Kelly Road to Colonial Avenue and on to Breakneck Hill Road in Middlebury, before coursing onto Charcoal Avenue and White Deer Rocks Road.

**The Richardsons would entertain American troops in this
house during the War of revolution (R. Sullivan photo)**

Ebenezer's fifth son, also Nathaniel, after his deceased brother,
inherited the original homestead down in the valley east of Three Mile
hill near the Moss road, after the death of his stepmother, Hannah. He
built a new house there about 1750. [62]According to legend, Nathaniel kept
a tavern there, and married Phoebe Brounson, daughter of John Brounson,
on April 1, 1752. From the genealogy of John Bronson, (Brounson) as
recorded in Anderson, we see that, in point of fact, Phoebe would have
been Nathaniel's stepsister.

One can only imagine the excitement of the Richardson family and,
no doubt, most of the residents of Breakneck, when a tall, swarthy General,
in blue and buff uniform, astride a chestnut bay, stopped at their home on
the woodbury road in 1780 or 1781. Anderson writes, in a footnote, that:
"Here, tradition tells us, that General Washington dined on one occasion,
his horse, meanwhile, being made fast to an enormous elm tree, lately
standing (1896) in front of the inn." [63] One wonders whether delegate John
Adams and his party may have stopped here for a bit of libation back in

---

62 BRD, p. 5.
63 AND, p. 554. Footnote.

January 1777, before continuing his rough ride up Breakneck Hill. More on this later, as well.

Moses Bronson, yet another son of Isaac, the planter, apparently also owned a home in the vicinity of Bronson's Meadow, (the area around the Memorial Middle School) which he sold to his brother Ebinezer, in 1729. This property was sold in exchange, just 6 years later to one William Judd. He could not have lived at Breakneck for very long if at all, because the property was soon in the hands of the Ebinezer Richardson mentioned above. [64]

Isaac, the planter (serg. brunson, as he was then known) figured prominently in the early settlement of Mattatuck [Waterbury]. On October 7, 1703, he, together with Thomas Judd and Edmund Scott, were chosen " *t' provide what was needful for the entertaining the elders and messengers of the ordaining Mr. [John] Southmayd,*" first Minister to the parish at Mattatuck. The ordination did not, however, take place for a few more years. Thus, Isaac Bronson more than likely established a house on Breakneck before the first meetinghouse in Mattatuck was constructed. (on the east end of the present green, where the Carrie Welton fountain now stands)

At least three of his sons served the colony, in Waterbury's train band. Some time after 1721, Isaac II served first as corporal then as sergeant in the First Company of militia, while his brother, Thomas, served as Lieutenant when the Second Company was formed in 1732. In 1740, another son, John, served as Lieutenant, when a Third Company was formed. It is probable that the brothers may also have seen service during King Phillip's War.

In December of 1738, a vote of the Proprietors was passed that school monies be divided among the different Societies "according to their lists of estate." In December of 1749, the First Society was divided into four districts, for school purposes: the Town Plot, [Waterbury Center] Buckshill, Judd's Meadow and Breakneck. Each district (provided fifteen scholars were enrolled) would be provided for in proportion "of schooling and school money."

---

64 BRD, p. 5.

**The original Breakneck School located opposite the Watertown
Road (Middlebury Historical Society collection)**

At some point during the period between 1703 and 1771, a burying
ground was likely established in the area of Breakneck. A later reference to
"the southeast corner of the second lot opposite and north of the James C.
Tyler residence" (perhaps near the original site of the Bronson homestead)
places this first burying ground somewhere near the intersection of
Breakneck Hill Road and the present Tyler Crossing. That is, on the north
side of the former. This mystery is discussed in a later chapter.

Breakneck was not the only area of Waterbury's wilderness to be
settled. Others had constructed homes at some distance from the town
center. Obadiah Richards, Jr. was the first known inhabitant of present
Watertown. John and Ephraim Warner settled on Bucks Hill. Samuel
Hikcox had "settled his house" in present-day Naugatuck, then known as
Judd's Meadow. However, aside from these few brave souls, most settlers
of what was to become Waterbury resided within earshot of the beating
of a drum, which would call them to meeting. For the benefit of those
adventurers who chose to live in the hinterlands, the call to meeting had
to be posted in public view several days before. In an emergency, of course,
timely contact would be impossible. These earliest of settlers were a stalwart
and venturesome lot.

Dr. Bronson tells us that, prior to 1720, there were less than a dozen
families living in the wilderness of West Farms, (Middlebury) Bucks Hill
(northeast Waterbury) and Judd's Meadow (Naugatuck). [65] At least five of
these families lived at Breakneck.

But others would also be granted land in present-day Middlebury,
during the latter part of the 17th and early part of the 18th Century; lands
set away from the area of Breakneck. And, in time, more houses would
eventually be built.

65 BRH, p. 243.

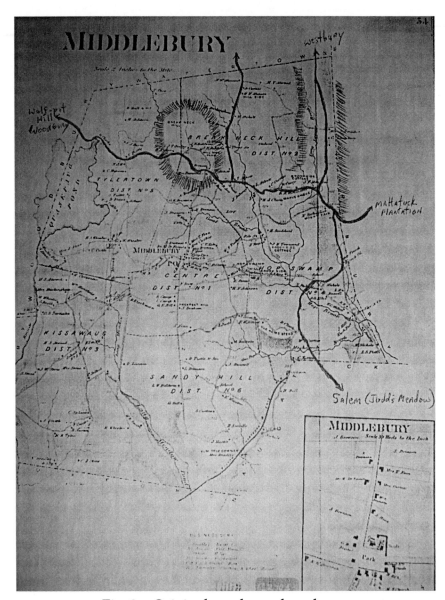

Fig. 2 – Original north-south and east-west routes through Breakneck

The first actual settler of Hop Swamp was either Ephraim Bissell or Dr. James Porter. Some, such as Dr. Porter, would construct their dwellings along a second route to Woodbury, laid out in 1720, which coursed along the present-day Whittemore Road, through what is now the center of the Town. It wound its way around Lake Quassapaug to the south, turned abruptly into the hollow of Eight Mile Brook, which was the main outflow of the lake, and followed the Old Woodbury (Sherman Hill) Road into Woodbury.

Dr. Porter constructed, about 1725, a timber frame house in the area known as Hop Swamp, that area named for its wild hops, which grew in abundance there. The house lay close to the little schoolhouse, once known as the Hop Swamp School. The exact location of this school remains unclear. Some suggest it may have been located on Meshaddock Road. (Shadduck Rd.) The Mary I. Johnson School, in relatively close approximation to the original site, later replaced it. The grant of land was originally given to brothers Dr. Daniel and Richard Porter, probably some time before 1700.

It was Richard's son, Dr. James, following in his uncle's footsteps, who settled there. After the house was torn down, a few years before 1896, a new one was constructed which was subsequently known as the Boughton place, just west of Old Regan Road. During the newer construction, it was noted that there was a "house within a house," a newer edition being built around the walls of the original.

The hill behind "the Boughton place" is known as Bissell Hill, so named for Ephraim Bissell of Tolland, who built there in 1728. That hill lies to the north of lower Whittemore Road. In 1740, Ephraim Bissell announced his going off to war in the Spanish West Indies, probably Cuba, against Spain. Regrettably, he never returned and was presumed killed there. The first mention of the area known as Hop Swamp [66] occurred as early as 1687, when George Scott received two grants of land there.

In 1735, Captain William Judd began the purchase of his "great farm," together with two houses and significant land stretching between Two and a Half Mile hill (along Straits Turnpike towards Watertown) and Three Mile hill. [67] The following year, Joseph Prime, of Woodbury, sold to Sergeant Moses Johnson of that town, two hundred nine acres near

---

66 So named for the abundance of wild hops which grew here and was used in the making of beer.

67 These hills were so named for the distance in which they lay from the town center of Waterbury.

Breakneck Hill. In 1737, James Porter sold to his brother Thomas, the Hop Swamp homestead of their father Daniel, "except 20 foot square on the east side, joining to the highway to build a small house upon." This was set aside for a Sabbath Day house, which was never constructed. The site on the present Green was selected some time later, as a more central location.

Abbott also tells us that "Deacon Timothy Porter's house was about one-fourth of a mile south from Dr. Porter's, probably on the old Moss road and his son, Mark Porter, had a house opposite the south end of [the present] Yale Avenue near his fathers." [68] Benjamin Bement "settled southwest of Hop Swamp between John and Timothy Porter's" in the area known as Meshaddock. [69] After the Great War, he moved to Wolcott, where he died.

Several individuals settled on what was once called Bedlam Hill, which ran south from the center of town. Some would build along the South Street, which led to Naugatuck, including Eliphat Bristol. Daniel Mallory, Samuel Umberfield, Jeremiah Peck and even further south, a Mr. Biscoe and Nathaniel Gunn.

John Thompson of Stratford was the first settler at Mount Fair, just below the intersections of routes 63 and 64, building a log house there in 1769.[70] Some time before this, Aaron Benedict came from Danbury and built a house on the corner of what are now Park Road and Straits Turnpike. This house burned down in 1916 but the rock wall around it can still be seen.

There were others, of course, who eventually settled in West Farms but the area known as Breakneck served as the main center of activity, until the development of the "town park," as the Middlebury Green was known, later in the 1700s.

---

68 BRD, p. 4.
69 Ibid.
70 BRD, p. 5.

Chapter III

The Bronson Legacy...

The singular name, which has become synonymous with present-day Middlebury and Breakneck in particular, is that of Bronson. While other families, such as the Warners, Richardsons, Judds and Abbotts settled at Breakneck, it was the descendants of Isaac and John Brounson, the original Mattatuck Planters, who developed most of the area. There are no less than one hundred individuals bearing that surname buried in the present Middlebury cemetery. The monumental work of Col. Herbert Bronson Enderton, an 8th generation descendant of John Bronson Jr., was printed in 1969. It literally chronicles thousands of descendents of the two Bronson brothers who settled in Middlebury. [71] In addition, numerous and oft times quite prominent Bronsons have spread from New York to as far away as Iowa, Michigan, Utah and California. The name appears in several diverse ways in the old records, to wit: "Brownson," "Brownsen," "Brunson," and even "Brounsen." But the Breakneck legacy begins with these two brothers.

Isaac Bronson (Isaak Brounson, srg. Brounson), the planter, the eighth child of John and Frances Hills Brounson of Farmington, was baptized by the Reverend Thomas Hooker, founder of the colony at Hartford, mentioned above, on December 7th, 1645. [72] He was one of the original Subscribers to the Articles of Settlement for the Mattatuck Plantation in 1673. His brother, John Jr., just a year older than Isaac, also removed with him to Mattatuck and became a bachelor-proprietor in 1674.

71 END, pp. 7-358
72 BRH, p. 138.

John Bronson Sr. of Farmington was the progenitor of all the Bronsons who inhabited Middlebury, and hence Breakneck, over the years. He died Nov. 28, 1680 and left an estate of £312. He had the following children:

1. Jacob: born in Jan. 1641, married Mary_____; left posterity and died in 1708. He lived in Farmington.
2. John Jr., the planter: born in Jan. 1644, to which we will allude later.
3. Isaac, the planter: born in Nov. 1645, baptized, as said, Dec. 7, 1645, in Hartford.
4. Mary: married an Ellis or Allis.
5. Abraham: baptized Nov. 28, 1647. He signed the Mattatuck articles, but declined the responsibilities of a planter. He removed to Lyme and married Hannah, daughter of Matthew Griswold and died at an advanced age.
6. Dorcas: married Stephen Hopkins of Hartford, father of John of Waterbury and died, May 13, 1697.
7. Sarah: married Ebenezer Kilbourn of Wethersfield.

FIRST GENERATION AT BREAKNECK

Isaac Bronson, the Planter, had his Mattatuck lot of four acres laid out on North Main Street in Waterbury, just a short distance from the northeast corner of the present Green, in the area of the former Waterbury Savings Bank. He was one of the original thirty subscribers to the Mattatuck plantation and was in the first company to come from Farmington. About 1695, he became a sergeant in the local train-band and was henceforth known as "Sergeant Bronson." [73] His wife Mary was the daughter of John Root[e] of Farmington. They were married there in 1669. His father, John Brounsen, may have come as one of the original settlers, with Rev. Hooker from Newtowne, Massachusetts Bay, to Hartford in 1636. Subsequently, John Bronson and his family removed to Tunxis (Farmington) in 1641, where Isaac and his brother, John Jr., another planter, were born. He was a petitioner with Mr. Jeremiah Peck to the General Court for liberty "to gather" a church and was one of its seven pillars of its final organization in 1691. [74]

---

73   Ibid. 140.
74   Ibid.

He granted a half-interest in his Waterbury estate to his son Ebinezer in 1714. The Proprietors' records suggest he probably built a house at Breakneck as early as April 6, 1702. Isaac and Mary had nine children:

1. Isaac Jr.: born in 1670 and died June 15, 1751. See below.
2. Lt. John: born in 1673 and died at the close of the year, 1746. "He is supposed to have lived first at Breakneck. He may have occupied the house of his father there in 1702. John had a house of his own there and twenty-two acres of land, Feb. 27th, 1705-06, which he bought, by exchange, of Joseph Gaylord, Sr. He later built a house on Cherry Street, near the corner of Walnut, in Waterbury.
3. Samuel: born about 1676. He was a cooper and lived in Kensington.
4. Mary: born Oct. 15, 1680, married Deacon Thomas Hickox and died in 1756.
5. Joseph: born in 1682 and died May 7, 1707.
6. Thomas: born Jan. 16, 1686 and died May 6, 1777. He was the fifth deacon of Waterbury's first church, his son being the sixth. He eventually lived in Waterbury.
7. Ebenezer: born in Dec. 1688. He was baptized in Farmington. Along with brothers Isaac, John, Joseph and Thomas, he was a bachelor-proprietor of Mattatuck.
8. Sarah: born Nov. 15, 1691 and died in 1748.
9. Mary: born Sept. 28, 1694 and married Richard Bronson of Woodbury. [75]

John Bronson, the Planter, brother of Isaac was also, as mentioned above, an original Mattatuck subscriber in 1674, as a bachelor-proprietor. Henry Bronson believes this John to be the brother of Isaac, above. His original plot was on the north side of west Main Street, probably in the area of the present YMCA and he was married to Sarah Ventris, who died on Jan. 6, 1711. John died in 1796. His estate amounted to £141, 6s.

There is no evidence that he or any of his offspring ever lived in the area, which was to become Middlebury.

They had the following children:

1. John: born in 1670; died June 15, 1716. He removed to Farmington and had several children.
2. Sarah: born in 1672.

---

75 Ibid. 141-42.

3. Dorothy: born in 1675; married Stephen Kelsey of Wethersfield. They deeded their right in her father's property to a son Stephen, who moved to Waterbury.
4. Ebenezer: born in 1677, married Mary Munn, Aug. 13, 1702 and died May 23, 1727. He lived and died in Woodbury.
5. William: born in 1682, married in 1707, Esther Barnes; he removed to Farmington at an early date.
6. Moses: born in 1686. Married Jane Wait of Stratford and died Aug. 12, 1754. Was a bachelor-proprietor in 1706-7 but moved to Stratford only to return to Waterbury in 1723. The couple had 13 children.
7. Grace: born in 1689.

SECOND GENERATION

Isaac Jr. Son of Isaac, the Planter. Henry Bronson tells us that Isaac [Jr.] "purchased (April 24, 1704) of Ephraim Warner a house and lot on the northwest corner of Cook and Grove Streets where he perhaps lived for a time. He owned land at Breakneck hill at an early date. In June 1701, he purchased of Thomas Warner twelve acres on the south side of the Woodbury road. He went there to live before March, 1707 and is considered as the first permanent settler of what is now Middlebury." [76] He was a bachelor-proprietor, a delegate to the General Assembly in 1723 and 1733 and was a highly respected and influential gentleman of the town for many years. Isaac Jr. married Mary Morgan in 1701. She died in 1749, two years before her husband. They too had nine children:

1. Jerusha: born Nov. 8, 1703 probably in Waterbury, married Paul Welch of New Milford and likely removed there.
2. Isaac III: born Mar. 29, 1707, according to tradition, the first child born in the present town of Middlebury. See below.
3. Anna: born Aug. 23, 1709, married 1st Daniel How, 2nd Isaac Tuttle.
4. Josiah [Lt.]: born June 6, 1713. He built on Breakneck hill, in 1738, the oldest existing house in present-day Middlebury. See below.
5. Mary: born May 29, 1716, married James Hine of New Milford.
6. Nathan: born May 29, 1719 and died on Dec. 4, 1722.
7. James: born Oct. 27, 1721 and died 1725.

---

76 Ibid. p. 141.

8. Patience: born Apr. 14, 1725 and married Stephen Hopkins, a distant relative, on Oct. 11, 1744. She died on June 3, 1746.
9. James: born Oct. 22, 1727 and died on Apr. 15, 1826. He married Deborah Abbott Brocket of Wallingford and had six children. He was a veteran of the Revolutionary War.

THIRD GENERATION

Isaac Bronson III, as previously noted, was the first child born at Breakneck, on the 27th or 29th of March in 1707. This fact is indicated on his tombstone. Of interest also, is the other prognostic inscription carved in stone, there:

Hark! From the tomb, a doleful sound
Your ears attend the cry
Ye living men come view the ground
Where you must shortly lie.

His home, as was also noted, was probably where the James C. Tyler homestead exists, just up the Breakneck Hill road from Tyler Crossing, on the south (left hand) side of the road. Isaac III married Eunice, daughter of Thomas Richards on July 3, 1734, and she died on Sept. 6, 1749. He married, 2nd, Abigail Brocket, widow of Caleb Munson Nov. 22, 1750. Isaac III died on Dec. 7, 1799 at age 93. There is a record of Isaac being fined, in 1737, the amount of five shillings for violating the Sabbath-day law against performing "servile labor." His offense was in allowing his sister to ride upon his horse behind him on a Sunday night after the meeting. [77]

Isaac III served in the Revolutionary war and it was at his home that Lafayette stopped and Rochambeau was quartered in 1781.

With Eunice, Isaac Jr. had the following children:
1. Lois: born Jan. 26, 1735, married Isaac Prichard of Waterbury.
2. Capt. Isaac [IV]: born Oct. 2, 1736, inherited the original homestead. See below.
3. Hannah: born Jan. 31, 1738-39, married Timothy Clark.
4. Lydia: born June 29, 1741 and died Sept. 6, 1749, on the same day as her mother.
5. Eli: born June 30, 1743.
6. Patience: born Dec. 12, 1746 and also died on Sept. 6, 1749.

---

77 Enderton, Col. H.B.: Vol. I, p. 90

7. Seth: born Dec. 7, 1748.

8. Titus: born Oct. 15, 1751. See below.

With his second wife, Abigail he had:

9. Abigail: born on Aug. 12, 1753, who in turn married Ambrose Hickox.

It is curious that Isaac's first wife, Eunice, then age 33, together with their daughters, Lydia, age 8 and Patience, almost 3, all died the same day. This would suggest some tragic accident, as opposed to a form of disease. One of the major killers of women of the 17th and 18th centuries was **fire.**

Lt. Josiah Bronson, Son of Isaac Jr. and Mary Morgan and brother to Isaac III, figured prominently in the history of early Breakneck, also. He was a lieutenant in the local militia. He married Dinah, daughter of John Sutliff, on July 23, 1735. She died Sept. 10, 1736 in childbirth. Josiah built his house on the great curve of Breakneck hill in 1738 and it still stands, as the oldest house in Middlebury. He married, second, Sarah Hurd, widow of David Leavenworth of Woodbury, on May 15, 1740 and welcomed her into a brand new home. Josiah married, third, Rebecca, widow of Moses Hurlbut of Woodbury, on Dec. 23, 1767, just four months after Sarah died. Lastly, he married his fourth wife, another widow, Huldah Williams, on June 12, 1798. Henry Bronson describes Josiah as "blest by nature with a robust constitution, a cheerful, buoyant spirit and an iron will" which set him in good stead to "grapple with the many difficulties incident to the times in which he lived." [78] He also tells us that he secured wealth, and obtained an honorable position in society. The Josiah Bronsons graciously entertained Rochambeau's second in command, Baron de Vioménil, in 1781. Josiah died on Feb. 20, 1804, at the ripe old age of 91. He had the following children:

With his first wife, Dinah:

1. Lucy was born on Sept. 10, 1736 but, although her mother died giving birth, Lucy survived. She married James Porter of Hop Swamp, in Middlebury on Nov. 9, 1762.

Following Josiah's marriage to Sarah, they had:

2. David: born June 25, 1741. He married Anna Porter, daughter of Dr. Daniel Porter and sister of James above, on March 1, 1772.

3. Abel: born May 30, 1743, a physician who would later figure prominently in the introduction of Small poxe inoculation to Middlebury. (See subsequent chapter.)

---

78 Ibid. p. 470.

4. Zuba (Azubah): born Apr. 28, 1745, who would marry Abner Munson.
5. Ruben (Reuben): born June 5, 1747. He married Jemima (Jennie) Porter, daughter of Lt. Samuel Porter on Nov. 1, 1770.
6. Thaddeus: born on July 22, 1749. He married, first, Abigail Wilmot on Dec. 10, 1772. She died on May 25, 1793 and he married, second, Anne Hitchcock on Jan. 5, 1794.
7. Josiah, Jr.: born Feb. 1, 1751-2, who would build his home just over the hill to the west, from his parents. He married Tabitha Tuttle, daughter of Ezekial Tuttle of Middlebury on Jan. 20, 1780. Josiah Jr. was a Private in Capt. Hill's Co., Bradley's Battalion, of Wadsworth's Brigade during the war of Revolution.
8. Elijah: born May 15, 1755. He was married to Lois Bunnell, daughter of Stephen Bunnell of Wallingford on March 10, 1778. He too served in the War of Revolution and died on March 17, 1822.

**Lt. Josiah Bronson built upon Breakneck in 1738
(with permission of Richard Seman family)**

FOURTH GENERATION

Captain Isaac Bronson - Eunice Richards Bronson would not live long enough to see her son, Isaac IV, distinguish himself in the War of Revolution. Nor would she see any of her grandchildren. The Captain would marry Mary, daughter of Josiah Brocket of Wallingford on Feb. 13, 1755 and they would have nine children together. He died on Apr. 15, 1826, at age 90 and is buried in the Middlebury Cemetery. His service to his country is chronicled in another chapter of this work. They lived in the old homestead on the south side of Breakneck Hill Road, which he inherited from his father. Their children include:

1. Eunice: born Dec. 4, 1755 and died Oct. 10. 1777. (See next chapter)
2. Mary: born Sept. 15, 1757 and married Eblem Hill and moved to Ohio.
3. Isaac V: born Mar. 10. 1760. See below.
4. Laban: born Feb. 14, 1762, died 1801.
5. Ethel: born July 22, 1765. See below.
6. Chauncey: born Dec. 31, 1767 and died in 1768.
7. Hannah: born in May of 1769 and married Eli Hine on Oct. 30, 1792.
8. Sarah: born March 21, 1775 and died Oct. 10, 1777. (See next chapter)
9. Virtue: born March 22, 1778, married Nancy Carrington, and died in 1815 in Ontario Co. New York.

Titus Bronson, half-brother of Capt. Isaac, also saw military service during the war of Revolution. His service is also discussed in a subsequent chapter. He enlisted as a Private in 1775 and re-enlisted in Capt. Obed Foote's Company in 1781. Titus married Hannah, daughter of Moses Cook on Feb. 11, 1799, during the period of his military service. They would have eight children. A daughter, Sally, born in 1794, would marry Albe Benham and remain in Middlebury. Titus would die on Aug. 14, 1829 at only 38 years of age.

Dr. Abel Bronson, son of Josiah and Sarah Leavenworth Bronson, was born on May 30, 1743. He married, first, Lydia Benham, with whom he had two children and second, Esther Hawkins, with whom he had six more. He was an early member of the state Medical Society. In 1782, Abel was one of only three physicians in the Waterbury First Society. The others were Isaac Baldwin of Naugatuck and Preserved Porter. [79] He too may have studied under Dr. Lemuel Hopkins of Hartford. He served in the War of Revolution. He may have lived in a house, which lay just west of Mirey Dam Road, where it meets the upper reaches of the old Burr Hall Road. In 1778, we know that Dr. Bronson was in Middlebury attending a sick soldier, as is evidenced by the fact that he was allowed *"a bill for Docktring a sick soldier who lived at Lieut. Bronson's."* [80] His "poxe house" was located near his home, some time after 1784, as described in a subsequent chapter. He later removed to Woodbury, where he died on Aug. 2, 1805 and is buried in Watertown.

FIFTH GENERATION

Henry Bronson tells us that **Dr. Isaac Bronson V;** son of Capt. Isaac and Mary Brocket Bronson first pursued the study of medicine as a youth, with Dr. Lemuel Hopkins of Hartford. [81] He entered the army as a junior surgeon in the War of Revolution, on the 14th of November 1779, in the 2nd regiment of light dragoons, commanded by Col. Elisha Sheldon, in the Connecticut Line.

Johnson reveals that Dr. Bronson was a member of the: "Society of the Cincinnati, 1783" [82] This rather select society was established to preserve the ideals and fellowship of Revolutionary War officers. He was ultimately promoted to senor surgeon and served to the end of the war. At the close of the war, Mr. Bronson abandoned the field of medicine and travelled to India and Europe, returning in 1789. On his return to the states, he settled in Philadelphia by 1792 then removed to New York, where he became a prominent businessman and banker. He ultimately moved his business to Bridgeport, where he opened a bank in 1807. He lived most of the year at Greenfield Hill in Stratford, where he died on July19, 1839. The couple had ten children.

Ethel Bronson, a younger brother of Dr. Isaac, was born in Breakneck on July 22, 1765. He married, Dec. 30, 1787, Hepzibah, daughter of Joseph Hopkins, Esq. Anderson tells us that "he became a prominent citizen of

79   AND, p. 486.
80   Ibid. p. 448.
81   Ibid. p. 371.
82   Ibid. p. 376.

his native town, was a justice of the peace and [like his father before him] a member of the Legislature for six sessions." [83] In May of 1804, he removed to Jefferson County, New York and became an agent of his brother, Dr. Isaac, for the sale of lands. He then served three terms in the New York state Legislature and became a judge of the County Court. At the time of his death, in 1825, he was President of Jefferson County Bank.

Silas Bronson, son of Elijah and Lois Bunnell Bronson and grandson of Lieut. Josiah, was born on Feb. 15, 1788. Dr. Anderson tells us that he was born to farming and to moderate means. After a simple district education, he became a carpenter and joiner for four years, before moving to Georgia, where he spent the next fifteen years as a merchant. His success led him to remove to New York in 1830, where he made his fortune in importing and jobbing dry goods, despite a setback during the great fire of 1835. Silas never married and willed some $200,000 to the Town of Waterbury for founding a library there. It is now named in his honor. [84]

Leonard Bronson Esq., son of Titus and Hannah Cook Bronson, was born at Breakneck on June 24, 1797. He was educated at Breakneck district school. Leonard received the property on Breakneck Hill Road from his brothers and sisters, by quitclaim, in December of 1841. [85] In 1848, Leonard was elected to the State Legislature from the 5th District and also served as Deacon of the First Church. He was the first Treasurer of the Savings Bank and Building Association of Waterbury, when it was established in April of 1852. In the following year, he was elected President and served until 1857. He also served as Moderator, because of his position as senior Justice of the Peace, of the first meeting of the Waterbury city council under the new Charter, on the first Monday of July in that year of 1853. [86] He was married to Nancy Richardson, daughter of Nathaniel Richardson Jr. and Comfort Stone on Apr. 14, 1819.

Titus Bronson Jr., older brother of Leonard, was born at Breakneck on Nov. 27, 1788. Middlebury church records indicate that he was married here in 1825, by the Rev. Mark Reed. Others suggest that he married Sally Richardson on Jan. 1, 1827. [87] He removed to Ann Arbor, Michigan and

83   AND, p. 374, ap.
84   Ibid. p. 1013.
85   Middlebury Land Records, V.5, p. 457.
86   AND, V. II, p. 37.
87   Enderton, Col. H.B.: Vol. I, p. 94

thence to Davenport, Iowa as an early settler there. In 1829, Titus was the first white settler to build a cabin within the present city limits of what is now Kalamazoo, Michigan. He platted the town in 1831 and named it the village of Bronson. He was frequently described as "eccentric" and argumentative and was later run out of town. The village of Bronson was renamed Kalamazoo in 1836 (due in part to an incident resulting in Bronson's being fined for stealing a cherry tree). Today, a hospital and a park, among other things, are named after Titus Bronson.

After leaving Kalamazoo, Bronson found his way to Davenport, Iowa, where, in 1842, he lost most of his money in a land swindle. His wife also died in that same year. Bronson lived in Illinois for a short while, and then returned to Breakneck, by then known as Middlebury, where he died on Jan. 5, 1863, a broken man. His headstone reads: "A Western Pioneer, Returned to Sleep with his Fathers."

SIXTH GENERATION

Isaac Hopkins Bronson was born in Waterbury, the parish of Middlebury, on Oct. 16, 1802. He was predeceased by two years, by a brother, also named Isaac, who lived only 4 months. This Isaac removed with his father, Ethel, and mother, Hepzibah, and his three surviving siblings, to Rutland, Jefferson Co., New York in 1804. He was admitted to the bar in1822, rose rapidly in his profession and was elected to the twenty-fifth Congress of the United States in 1836. He served in the House of Representatives from 1837 to 1839. He later removed to St. Augustine, in what was to become the state of Florida in 1840 and was appointed United States Judge for the Eastern District there. [88] He died on Aug. 13, 1855 in Palatka, Florida.

Edward Leonard Bronson was also born at Breakneck, to Leonard Bronson and Nancy Richardson on January 18, 1828. Edward attended the Breakneck district school and schools in Pittsford, New York. After a short stint at teaching, he moved to Waterbury in 1848. There, he briefly joined his brother Isaac, above, in a stationery manufacturing firm aptly called "Bronson Brothers." When this business faltered, he joined the firm of Benedict & Burnham and eventually rose to the position of Treasurer. Later, he became a director of the Waterbury Watch Company,

---

88 AND, p. 375, ap.

the forerunner of Middlebury's Timex Corporation, and became its' Treasurer as well.

In October of 1861, Edward married Sarah Cornelia, daughter of Charles Townsend of Middlebury. They had a daughter, Julia Maria, and lost a son in infancy. Eventually the couple would adopt Sarah's nephew, Charles Bradley Pardee, who took his new parents' surname. Edward served in many civic capacities including alderman and councilman and in 1857, succeeded his father as Deacon of the First Church. Leonard died in Waterbury July 20, 1890. [89]

Capt. Isaac Richardson Bronson, another son of Leonard and Nancy, was born in Middlebury in 1826. On Oct. 22, 1851, he married Louisa M. Bronson, a distant cousin and daughter of Capt. Philo Bronson then of Geneva, New York and granddaughter of Eli and Mehitabele Atwater Bronson of Middlebury. Both Capt. Isaac and his wife Louisa are descended from Isaac Bronson III.

This Capt. Isaac served admirably in the War Between the States as a soldier with the 11th Connecticut Volunteers. This regiment was led by Col. Griffin A. Stedman of Hartford and became a part of Union Maj. Gen. Joseph Hooker's Army of the Potomac. Regrettably, Isaac was mortally wounded while fighting at the Battle of Chancellorsville. This battle was waged in Spotsylvania County, Virginia, from April 30th to May 6th 1863 and resulted in a major defeat at the hands of General Robert E. Lee's Army of Northern Virginia. He gave up his life for his country at Potomac Creek, Virginia, just a month later, on June 2, 1863. His remains were returned for burial in the Middlebury Cemetery. Of interest is the fact that General Thomas "Stonewall" Jackson was also mortally wounded in the same battle.

Dr. Oliver Bronson, son of Isaac V and Anna Olcott Bronson, was born at Breakneck on Oct. 3, 1799. He was named after an older brother, who had died in infancy. He attended Yale University and graduated from the College of Physicians and Surgeons (later Columbia) in 1818. He toured France in his youth and did very well at investing his trust funds, mostly in railroads. Oliver married Joanna Donaldson of North Carolina on May 15, 1833 at the Murray Street Presbyterian Church in New York. For a time, the couple would live in Hudson, New York and had four children. From 1851 to 1854, Dr, Bronson served as Superintendent of

---

89   Ibid. p. 313.

Schools in Hudson, there in Columbia County. After a new Constitution was established by the new state of Florida in 1868, Bronson was hired, for some as yet unknown reason, by the new Governor Harrison Reed, to serve as the new St, John's County School System in November of that year. The family moved to a house in St. Augustine, which later became the Saint George's Hotel. He died in Richfield Springs, New York on July 21, 1875 at the age of 76.

There are countless other stories of successful Bronsons but, interestingly enough, none of the offspring remain in Middlebury. It is quite obvious, however, that the earliest settlers of Breakneck, in west Farms of Waterbury, have left a legacy, which is unsurpassed by any other family in this town to the present day.

Chapter IV

May They Rest in Peace...West Farms Earliest Cemetery

Sometime during the year 1771, the select men of Waterbury, Dr. Joseph Anderson notes, were appointed "to go and view and find a convenient place for a Burying place in the west part of the First Society." [90] The site chosen was "the first place of burial in Middlebury." However, in all likelihood, that site, on Breakneck Hill road, was already in use as a burial ground well before 1771.

G. Fred Abbott, writing in 1930, as included in "A History of Middlebury" by Delia Bronson, wrote: *"Our first cemetery, serving the settlement from 1703 to 1793 was in the southeast corner of the second lot opposite and north of James Tyler's house."* [91] This would place that cemetery almost opposite Tyler Crossing, upon Breakneck Hill Road. Some seniors may remember this lot as belonging to McDonald's farm.

Abbott continues: *"Many of the old stones were standing until about 1880 when James C. Scovill, the owner at that time, took up the stones and plowed the field. Two or three stones had been moved to the present cemetery. A peach orchard was set out there later."* [92] The Records of the Town of Middlebury indicate that Scoville purchased the property, on Feb. 6th, 1871 from Scoville Merrill Buckingham. [93] James Clark Scovill [e] was born in Waterbury in Sept. of 1826, a son of Edward Scovill and Harriet Clark. He

---

90 AND, p. 408.
91 BRD, p. 7.
92 Ibid.
93 Middlebury Land Records, V. 10: p. 149.

married Marcia Smith on the 20th of November 1850 in Middlebury and they had four children here. We also know that Buckingham was the son of Betsy Scovill, a distant cousin of James C. and John Buckingham. Scoville Buckingham had married Charlotte Ann, daughter of Aaron Benedict of Middlebury, in 1835. There is no evidence that Buckingham ever lived in this town, since he received the property from Charles Benedict in April 1870 [94] and held it for less than a year. This was probably one and the same property, on the north side of the "woodbery" road, which was granted to Isaac Bronson, the planter, as far back as 1702. The heirs of James Clark Scovill conveyed the property where the burial ground was located to Leavings Abbott, father of G. Fred Abbott, in 1887. [95]

Another one and one-forth acre of adjacent land was added to Scovill's holdings, from James E. Baldwin on Sep. 15th, 1781. [96] He lived near the junction of Artillery and Breakneck Hill Roads.

In her *Genealogy of the Judd, Abbott and Tyler Families of Middlebury, Ct.* compiled in 1984, produced by the Middlebury Historical Society, Claire Rice alludes to the fact that Stephen Abbott, who came with his wife, Hannah Frisbie, to Breakneck from Branford about 1750 and lived in "a small house on the north side of the road [Breakneck Hill] some 600 feet west of the Breakneck School corner." She writes that Stephen died at an advanced age and "was probably buried in the old cemetery some 800 feet northwest of his house." This would place the location of this early cemetery some 1400 feet west and slightly north of the old schoolhouse, or roughly opposite of where Tyler Crossing meets Breakneck Hill Road.

In reference to the present-day cemetery Abbott writes: *"In 1793 a half acre of the present cemetery was secured from Marcus Bronson and in 1842 another half acre was added on the west side. In 1871 the large tract at the north was added."*

"The [Middlebury] Cemetery was owned and cared for by the town until 1928 when the Middlebury Cemetery Association was incorporated and took over the management.

Mr. Eli Bronson was almost a life-long member of the Cemetery Committee and when the association was formed, his children bought and presented to the Association a large tract on the west side of the old grounds." [97]

---

94   Ibid. Vol. 10, p. 125.
95   Ibid. Vol. 11, pp. 287-88.
96   Ibid. p. 171.
97   BRD, p. 7.

This Account is only partly accurate. The author has noted that there are currently at least six stones (not two or three) in the present cemetery, located in the area referred to on the Middlebury Cemetery Map as Section V, which predate the existence of that cemetery. Section V is the oldest section, corresponding to the property conveyed by Marcus Bronson in 1793. One can only conclude that the stones were moved there from elsewhere and the Breakneck cemetery is obviously the most likely origin. These six stones differ from the remainder of the others set there, both in composition and color. They are of a reddish brownstone. Two of these markers were those of children, set to either side of their mother, Mary Bracket Bronson. She was the daughter of Josiah Bracket of Wallingford, who married Capt. Isaac Bronson, [IV] on 13 Feb 1755 and died 1 Aug 1816, ae. 76. Captain Isaac's stone lies nearby. He was born to Isaac Bronson III and Eunice Richards [on], daughter of Thomas Richards [on], at Breakneck, on 2 Oct 1736 and died 15 Apr 1826, ae. 90. The two smaller brown stones are those of his daughters:

"*Miss Eunice, eldeft Daughter to Capt. Isaac Brownfon,*" [according to the marker] and [according to Anderson born 4 Dec 1755 [98]] "*died 30 Jan 1776 in her 21ft year.*"

"*Sarah, Dau,'tr to Capt. Isaac Brownfon*" [born, according to Anderson, 21 Mar 1775(1776) [99]] "*and died Octo'r 10, 1777 in Ae. 2 years.*"

Two Stones in the present cemetery, belonging to two Bronson daughters, whose deaths predate the cemetery's existence (R. Sullivan photo)

98 AND, Appendix, p. 25.
99 Ibid.

The remaining stones we might call "cenotaphs," since it is likely they too mark empty graves, are as follows:

"Ezra Burjess, Son of Ezra Burjess late Dec'd died March 25th 1775 in his 3rd year."

"In Memory of Silvia Thompson, Daughter of Mr. Caleb Thompson, of Walingford And who Died September 21, 1793, Ae. 17"

"In Memory of Asa, Son to Mr. [Deac.] Seth Bronson who died March 11th 1791 in the 2d year of his age." Deacon Seth Bronson was the uncle of the above-named Eunice and Sarah, hence this Asa would be their first cousin.

"In Memory of Abigale [nee Wilmot*] Bronson the Wife of Mr. Thaddeus Bronson who Died May 25, AD 1793 the 43th Year of her age."* Thaddeus was the son of Josiah Bronson, whose house still stands on Breakneck. He and Abigale were married 10 Dec 1772. She died just eight days after the birth of their seventh child, Ruth, no doubt of childbed fever.

There are other stones in the present cemetery, differing from the above in composition and color but similar to surrounding stones perhaps of granite, which also may predate this cemetery's existence. These include:

"Polly Beecher, wife of John, died Feb. 2, 1793, age 19 years."

"Alfred Bronson, son of Ethel and Hapsey, born Oct. 13, 1791, died April 6, 1792."

"Thankful Smith, daughter of Capt. Ebenezer and Mrs. Thankful, died Dec. 29, 1793, age 31 years."

The question, which requires resolution in order to confirm the above probabilities, is whether the present burial ground was in use prior to its actual transfer of ownership in 1794. If not, these stones may mark empty graves as well.

Anderson also tells us that the following vote, passed on January 27, 1794, seems to refer to the present Middlebury Cemetery: *"voted that the petition of M. eli Bronson, praying for the burial ground in Middlebury Society, be referred to the selectmen [Waterbury] with power to grant said petition and make such compensation to the proprietor of said ground as they think best."* [100] Thus, it is quite evident that at least some of the above referenced tombstones could not have been original to the present cemetery.

At some time before July of 1959, however, during excavations for removal of soil on the north side of Breakneck Hill Road, near its intersection with Tyler Crossing, human remains were discovered. Lawrence Atchison recalls unearthing them on a portion of the old Mc Donald farm, which

---

100 AND, p. 679.

occupied the corner of Breakneck Hill and Watertown Roads. A photo of these remains, held in a box, by then First Selectman Raymond Messenger, appears in the 150th Anniversary Commemorative Booklet of the Town. The caption under the photo indicates that the bones were buried beneath the two Bronson daughters' headstones. However, examination of the photograph clearly indicates that the remains were those of adults, probably male, and not children – the length of the femur suggesting a very tall person at that.

Human remains found at Breakneck in 1959, no doubt from the original cemetery. They are shown here by then First Selectman Ray Messenger. (from the Middlebury Historical Society collection)

Life-long Middlebury resident Stephen Foss and Richard Proulx, formerly of Middlebury, recall having seen "a box of bones" over a number of years, stored in one of the old Police station jail cells, when the department was located in the basement of Town Hall. Foss remembers seeing such a box there well after the above date of burial. He recalls the box being different from that in the photo and remembers them being moved to the old firehouse at the corner of Middlebury Road and Regan Road, possibly as recently as 1970 but he is not aware of their fate. Could there have been another mysterious set of human remains?

In contrast with the previously discussed Abbott view concerning our earliest cemetery, Dr. Joseph Anderson records that: *"The earliest place of Burial in Middlebury, laid out in 1771, has entirely disappeared. Two stones only, in the present graveyard, are known to have been removed from the older one,* [101] *those of two daughters of Captain Isaac and Mary (Bracket) Bronson, who died in 1776 and 1777.* [102] He was obviously unaware of the other stones, which exist there.

Anderson also makes another reference to Middlebury's earlier burying ground: *"In May of 1771, the First Society asked the General Assembly for the return of the monies that had been taken from it, but obtained no redress. In the same year, the selectmen were appointed 'to go and view and find a convenient place for a Burying Place in the west part of the First Society.' The site selected was the first place of burial in Middlebury."* [103]

There is clearly a discrepancy between Abbott's account and that of Doctor Anderson. What of the years between 1703 and 1771? What human remains still lay under the cold brown earth in the first settlement of Breakneck? Whose remains were taken up in July 1958 and re-interred in the present cemetery? And, furthermore, what of the fate of those individuals' remains, whose tombstones rest in that cemetery, yet could not possibly have been buried there? For, the present cemetery did not even exist until 1794! The answers to these and other questions concerning our earliest settlers may never be known, without further archaeological investigation. But one thing is certain. It is highly likely that the area at Breakneck was already in use as a cemetery, by the time it was "laid out," according to Anderson, "in 1771." Although a few West Farms residents are listed as interred in Waterbury's Grand Street Cemetery (now Library Park), early ancestors of the Bronson, Abbott and Richardson

---

101 The author has identified six stones, not two, as described above.
102 AND, p. 679.
103 Ibid. p. 408.

families, living in the area at the time, along with many others who shaped Middlebury's past, were no doubt interred at Breakneck.

In another entirely different yet unusual twist: on May 25th, 1931, a letter was directed to then First Selectman Howard Bronson, from John T. Monzani, Coroner for New Haven County at Waterbury, as follows:

In the matter of the articulated bones which were found within the precinct of the town of Middlebury on April 27th, 1931, this is to notify you that all the proceedings of Medical Examiner and Coroner in the matter of the investigation of said skeleton have terminated and in compliance with the statutes, Section 254 of the General Statutes, Revision of 1930 there being no friends to take charge, you are directed as first selectman of the town, to bury them.

Very truly yours,
John T. Monzani (signature)
Coroner for New Haven County,
At Waterbury

Appended to this letter was a hand-written note stating:

The afore referred bones were interred in Middlebury Cemetery 5/26/31 – a record of which will be found in Middlebury Cemetery records -----

This was signed " H A Bronson." The precise location where this skeleton may have been found has not been determined.

Chapter V

Mystery of the Skull

Stories abound concerning the Breakneck area, such as the tale elucidated above. For some, such as the author, they have captured the imagination, over the years. For others, they may be entirely unknown. But none is more fascinating or more macabre, than that surrounding the grave of Hannah Cook Bronson, wife of Titus Bronson, whose remains lie in the present Middlebury Cemetery.

Hannah was born to Moses Cook and Sarah Culver, on the northeast corner of Cook and Grove Streets in Waterbury, on June 10, 1755. She was later married to Titus Bronson, son of Isaac III and Eunice Richards Bronson of Breakneck. The couple had eight children here, including the Honorable Leonard Bronson, 5th District representative to the Legislature and Titus Bronson Jr., the founding settler of what was to become Kalamazoo, Michigan, both mentioned above.

It seems that on the evening of Dec. 7, 1771, her father, for whom Cook Street in Waterbury is named, was visiting David Clark's tavern in Bethany. Why he was there no one knows. A Mohegan Indian named Moses Paul, who was born in Barnstable, Massachusetts in 1742, was likewise present there at the tavern. Paul lived in Windham, Connecticut until he reached age 20. He then enlisted in the Provincial service in the regiment of Col. Israel Putnam and served admirably, during the French and Indian War. After the campaign was over, he took to the sea for several years and, as Samuel Orcutt writes in his History of Derby, "he became confirmed in bad habits." [104] Thus, once again, while at Clark's tavern

---

104 ORC, p. lxviii.

that lethal night, Paul had too much to drink and, when refused further service, took a swipe at proprietor Clark with a heavy flatiron, allegedly weighing some four and a half pounds. Paul would later, at trial, refer to it as "a stick or clubb." But, instead of hitting Clark, Paul's blow struck Moses Cook in the head, smashing his skull. Cook was carted back to his home in Waterbury, where he died five days later, on December 12th.

The story gets even more arcane. For some strange reason, Moses Cook's skull was not buried with his body. Instead, it was severed from it and prepared for examination. We do not know who may have prepared it, however. The skull was then exhibited as evidence at the trial of Paul, who would promptly be found guilty and sentenced to be hung until dead, in June of 1772. The execution was delayed, through a reprieve of three months, by the General Assembly, until December 17th of that year, when the sentence would be carried out in New Haven.

At Paul' request, the sermon was preached by one Sampson Occum, missionary to the Native Americans of the region. He took his sermon from the biblical text: "For the wages of sin is death but the gift of God is eternal life through Jesus Christ the Lord." [105]

So what, one may ask, does this all have to do with Breakneck? Well, it seems that after the trial was over, the skull of Moses Cook was returned to the family. It was for many years in the possession of Hannah Cook Bronson, here in Middlebury. She reportedly kept it (in several pieces) in a "little cloth bag" for some seventy-one years. At her request, the skull was buried with her in the present cemetery, in April of 1841. She was 86 years old at the time of her death. There is no indication on her tombstone of this unusual addition to her coffin.

Her grandson, Edward Leonard Bronson, a prominent Waterbury businessman and early Treasurer of the Benedict & Burnham Co., remembered seeing that little cloth bag on many occasions, in his grandparents' home. [106]

One can only imagine visiting Titus and Hannah at Breakneck and having the strange opportunity to gaze upon her father's smashed skull. Tread lightly, therefore, if your feet carry you to Section V, Range 11, and Lot 4 in the Middlebury Cemetery. There, Hannah sleeps for all eternity, under the watchful "eye" of her father.

---

105 Ibid. p. lxix.

106 See Chamberlain, Ava: *The Execution of Moses Paul: A Story of Crime and Contact in Eighteenth-Century Connecticut.* N.E. Quarterly, V. 77, No. 3: pp. 414-450 (Sep. 2004)

Chapter VI

The War of Conquest

Before the year of 1754, the French in Canada and their Native American allies, including the Algonquin, Ottowa, Shawnee and Ojibwa to the north, were stirring up trouble with the British colonists of New England, New York and Pennsylvania. In the same year, George Washington and some 400 men reached the Monongahela River in the Ohio territory and massacred a small French force. Some say this was the beginning of the war. He then established Fort Necessity there, which the French promptly overtook, with a much larger army. Washington surrendered on reasonable terms and returned to Virginia, rather embarrassed. He later acquitted himself somewhat, taking charge after the death of General Braddock, despite a resounding defeat and the French capture of Fort Duquesne. Early in 1755, the King put out a call to his colonies for "a considerable number of forces to be raised because of the invasion of his Majesty's just rights and dominions in North America, by the French and the Indians in their alliance." [107] The British had a strong alliance of their own, with the Iriquois nation. Sometimes referred to as "the War of Conquest," or "Guerre de la Conquête," this conflict came to be known as the more familiar "French and Indian War." The Native American role in this war is brilliantly captured in James Fennimore Cooper's *Last of the Mohicans*.

A number of individuals from West Farms answered the call of the King and fought in that war. New England was relatively spared of the fighting as the major battles took place largely in Pennsylvania, New York and in Canada. In the end, after the war drew to a close in 1763, resulting

---

107 AND, p. 389.

in a French defeat, both sides met in France. With the signing of the Treaty of Paris on February 15, 1763, most of present-day Canada was ceded to the British.

In that difficult year of 1755, the French were threatening from the north. Some one thousand men from Connecticut were called up for service. Local men known to have participated in the French and Indian War, from their burial inscriptions in the Middlebury Cemetery, included Eliphat Easton, Edward Smith and Abner Munson.

Other prominent West Farms names figuring strongly in the conflict include: Asa, John and Moses Bronson, Daniel Porter, who served as clerk to Capt. Eldad Lewis in the Fort William Henry alarm of 1757, and still others, such as Curtis, Fenn, Wooster, Barnes, Benham, Tuttle and Clark.

Among the West Farms residents who fought in that war were:

ABNER MUNSON – he was born on 8 Mar 1736 in what was then listed as Waterbury. He was the son of Caleb Munson and Abigail (Brocket) of Wallingford. He is listed as serving at Lake George under Captain Eldad Lewis , having "marched to the scene of danger in the 'Fort William Henry alarm' in 1757." [108] In August of that year, a French and Indian force, under Général de Montcalm, besieged Fort William Henry, situated at the head of Lake George in upstate New York and commanded by Lt.-Col. George Monro. The siege of the fort resulted in considerable casualties. But fortunately Munson was not amongst them. In March of 1762, he was again assigned to Captain Eldad Lewis' 7th Company of the 2nd Regiment as a Centinel, under Colonel Nathan Whitney. [109] [110] After leaving his Majesty's service, on 24 Sep 1764, he married Azubah, daughter of Josiah and Sarah Bronson of Breakneck Hill. Prior to his service, Abner added his name to a petition for winter privileges for the settlement at West Farms, along with his father-in-law and thirty others. The Munsons subsequently had 9 children, 6 boys and 3 girls, between the years of 1763 and 1788. Abner died on 2 Dec 1807 at the age of 72 years. He is buried with his wife and three of their children, Caleb and Lucinda, as well as Caleb's daughter Mary, who died at age 14, in the present Middlebury Cemetery.

ASA BROWNSON – served as Centinel in Capt. Israel Woodward's Waterbury Company, in the expedition against Crown Point, upon Lake

---

108 AND, p. 326
109 ACB, p. 333
110 AND, p. 397 suggests this was the First regiment under Col. Whiting.

Champlain, from April to December 1756. This was the Sixth Company of the Second regiment, and part of some 2500 Connecticut men, divided into four regiments of eight companies each. [111]

JOHN BROWNSON – son of John Brownson and Mary Hikcox, John was born on 23 April 1701, a grandson of Isaac the Planter. He too served as a Centinel in Woodward's Company, the Sixth Company of the Second regiment, at Crown Point, New York. [112]

MOSES BROWNSON – a nephew of Isaac the Planter and son of John the Planter and Sarah Ventris, may have lived briefly at Breakneck, in his younger years. Moses also served as Centinel in Woodward's company in 1756 and served yet again in the Second Regiment from March 27th to November 16, 1758. He was then commanded by Capt. Eldad Lewis and responded to the "Fort William Henry Alarm." [113]

ELIPHALET EASTON – Easton was the son of Joseph Easton and Susanna Burnham, was born 9 Aug 1732 and died 22 Jul 1811 at the age of 84. He was buried in the Middlebury Cemetery. His wife Mary died on 12 Dec 1812. The United States census of 1790 lists him as a resident of Woodbury at that time. Iris Guertin tells us that Easton was a member of Capt. John Marsh's Company, Col. Ebenezer Marsh's regiment, which was in service during the alarm and for the relief of Fort William Henry and parts adjacent." [114]

EDWARD SMITH – Smith died 29 July 1813 at 82 years of age. He was another signatory to the West Farms petition for winter privileges, filed for a second time with the General Assembly, in October of 1760. He was assigned to Captain Ebenezer Downs' company, in service during the alarm and for the relief of Fort William Henry in August of 1757. [115]

DANIEL PORTER – born on March 8, 1731 to Daniel Porter and Hannah Hopkins, he later became a doctor. Porter first served as company clerk, under Capt. Eldad Lewis, in the Fort William Henry alarm of 1757. He subsequently served at Crown Point in 1759, where he died at age 28 of the small-poxe. He never married. Little is known of him except "that his ability and skill were sufficient to justify his appointment and that he had the courage to accept it." [116]

---

111 Ibid. p. 392.
112 Ibid.
113 Ibid. p. 394.
114 ACB, p. 199.
115 Ibid. p. 204
116 AND, p. 833.

Chapter VII

Rumblings of Revolution

On June 1, 1774, in response to rebellious acts of the colonists against British taxation, in what would become known as "the Boston Tea Party," an English Parliament controlled by King George III issued the highly unpopular Boston Port Bill. This bill, in effect, completely blocked all trade in and out of Boston, save for His Majesty's ships. The bill also cut off vital supplies of sheep, cattle, hay and even wood, from the harbour islands around Boston, to the citizens of Boston and surrounds. This left the populace of that city in dire straits. On November 22, 1774, Waterbury responded to a general call for assistance, with the establishment of a Committee of Relief. This consisted of thirteen men, "appointed to receive donations contributed towards the relief of the poor in Boston." West Farms people responded in turn. James Porter, then living in the Hop Swamp region, served as a member that committee.

In that same year, all three of Waterbury's Militia Companies became part of Connecticut's Tenth Regiment, under Lt. Col. Jonathan Baldwin. Isaac Bronson IV was serving as Ensign of the First Militia Company, which became the Second Company of the Tenth Regiment. The Second Waterbury Militia Company became the Twelfth, under Captain Hezekiah Brown. Isaac Benham, son of Ebenezer, of West Farms, served as its Lieutenant.

Military assignments were somewhat confusing, during the period of that war. Early on, after the Battle of Bunker's Hill [117] in June of 1775, at Charlestown, Massachusetts, a number of surrounding colonies,

---

117 This famous battle was actually fought upon Breed's Hill.

Connecticut included, sent local militia companies to help support the brave men, who were keeping the British at bay, in the town of Boston. Those assignments were invariably of a short-term nature.

In July of 1775, when General George Washington assumed command of a new Continental Army in Cambridge, Congress required the colonies, to establish formal regiments, to help support the cause. The first of these regiments, consisting of eight such units formed in 1775, became known as the Connecticut or Continental Line. Eight more regiments were added in 1776 and a further eight, together with infantry, Dragoons and artillery units during the years of 1777 to 1781.

Considerable consolidation of the various regiments occurred during the years of 1781 through 1783. Many regiments were combined, renumbered or disbanded. Other regiments were more commonly referenced by the names of their commanders. Further, the Continental Army was divided into Northern and Southern Departments. All of this leaves the reader somewhat confused as to the precise assignments of many of those who served.

The following is a list of West Farms (Middlebury) men who fought on the side of the new Union, and who are buried in the old Middlebury Cemetery. It may not, by any means, be complete. Many of these men were born, grew up or lived at Breakneck, while others married Breakneck residents. It would be unfair to omit the others who did not have any connection to Breakneck, since they all contributed so much to the survival of this country. The facts are presented in their original form, as they appear in the references to this volume. A brief description of each of the major Connecticut regiments follows this list.

*****

AUGUSTUS PECK   1760 – 3 Jun 1812

Peck "Enl. [isted] December 14, 1776 – [for the] Duration of War."
[118] He served in the 5th Co. Capt. Jonas Prentice [of New Haven] 5th Batt. [alion of] Wadsworth's Brigade. [6th Regiment of the Connecticut Line] The "Battalion [was] raised June, '76 to reinforce Washington's army at New York. He served in the city (New York) and on the Brooklyn front, being at the right of the line of works during The Battle of Long Island, Aug. 27. Peck was then engaged in the retreat to New York Aug. 29-30; and stationed with a militia brigade under Col. Douglas at Kips Bay, 34th

---

118 HPJ, p. 214.

Street on the East River, at time of enemy's attack on New York, Sep. 15, and forced to retreat hurriedly. [He was] at Battle of White Plains, Oct. 28. Term expired Dec. 25, '76." [119] He later served in the "4th Regiment, Connecticut Line, 1781-83. Pd. from Jan. 1, '81 to Dec. 31, '81." [120]

Peck's burial Inscription in the Middlebury Cemetery reads as follows: "d. [suddenly] June 3, 1812, aged 52 years." [121] The military marker indicates that Capt. Augustus served in Capt. [David] Humphrey's Co.

EBENEZER SMITH   1730 – 9 Oct 1808

Smith served as a Private in "Capt. David Humphrey's [of Derby] Co., Col. Heman Swift's Connecticut Regiment, Feb. 11, 1783." [7th Regiment of the Connecticut Line, under the 2nd Connecticut Brigade, headed by Brigadier Gen. Jedediah Huntington] [122]

His burial Inscription reads: "Capt. Ebenezer, d. Oct. 9, 1808, aged 78 Yrs." [123] Delia Bronson tells us: "Ebenezer Smith [was] located at the outlet of Quassapaug about 1720." (N.b. – this may have been the father of the above Ebenezer) [124]

The Records of the Middlebury church reveal that he was "admitted to church membership Sep. 8, 1799 from Southbury. Vet. Rev. War, Mil Reg 1779." [125]

Later, Ebenezer Smith would be one of the petitioners to the General Assembly seeking the status of a separate town for Middlebury.

SIMEON MANVILLE   1760 – 17 Apr 1825

Henry Johnson, in his Record of Connecticut Men in the Revolution, tells us that Manville served in "Col. Roger Enos' (of Simsbury) State Rgt. June 1777. Minute Men and Volunteers, David Leavenworth, Capt. Horseneck [Greenwich] June 12, 1779. A pay abstract [exists] for Leavenworth's Co. in Col. Moseby's Regiment of militia in the State of Connecticut for guarding Horseneck under the command of Left. Col. Canfield." [126]

---

119 Ibid. p. 406-07.
120 Ibid. P. 337-40.
121 PRD, p. 317.
122 HPJ, p. 362.
123 PRD, p. 317.
124 PRD, p. 6.
125 SMB, p. S-14.
126 HPJ, p. 615.

His burial Inscription reads: 'd. April 17, 1825, aged 65 years." [127] The Middlebury census of 1820: p. 174, records his ID# as "CT52a793487."

Manville married Electa, daughter of Phineas Benham. Church records reveal that he was "Adm [itted]. June 9, 1800. Funeral April 18, 1825. Vet Rev War, Capt. Leavenworth's Co. Col. Moseley's Reg't." [128]

GIDEON PLATT   1754 – 22 Oct 1816

Platt was the son of Gedeon Platt Sr. and served as a private in "Capt. Peck's Co. [originally the 10th Company of the 1st Regiment] (Capt. Samuel Peck of Milford re-entered service in 1776) 3rd Co. 5th Batt. Wadsworth's Brigade, [under regimental commander,] Col. Douglas; 1776 Pvt. Pension, Mar. 4, 1831 at 77 years Ann. Allowance: 29, 66. [129] He married Hannah Clark, also of Milford, in March of 1783. [130]

His cemetery inscription reads: "d. Oct 22, 1816, aged 62 years," [131] while Middlebury church records simply state: "Vet. Rev. War. Capt. Peck's Co." [132]

His grandson, Dr. Gideon Lucien Platt, born in Middlebury July 20, 1813, would distinguish himself as President of the New Haven County and Connecticut State Medical Societies and as a co-founder of the Apothecaries Hall Co. in Waterbury.

BENJAMIN HINE, Sr.   1719 – 8 NOV 1800

While his son, Benjamin Hine, Jr., served the town in the War of 1812, Benjamin Sr. served in the War of revolution as a First Lieutenant in the "2nd Battalion, State Regiment under Gens. Spencer [2nd Regiment] and Wooster [1st Regiment]. [They] defended [the] Westchester border. [Officers included] Thaddeus Cook, Col., Epaphrus Sheldon, Lt. Col., Edw. Russell, Major, James Robinson, Capt." [133]

Johnson also tells us that Hine served in the "Militia under Gen. Gates to the northward, 1777," [probably around Boston] [134] and "Commands Guard at Milford foot in '77." [135] His title as Captain no doubt emanated

---

127 PRD, p. 317.
128 SMB, p. M-10.
129 HPJ, p. 408.
130 AND, p.
131 PRD, p. 317.
132 SMB. p. P-
133 HPJ, p. 424.
134 Ibid. p. 513.
135 Ibid, p. 629.

from his service in the local militia. These ranks did not carry over to the continental army.

Secretary of State Hinman compiled a list of men serving in the Revolution, in 1842. Hine's initial appointment by the General Assembly, in October of 1776 is listed thus: "Capt. Benjamin Hine was appointed ensign (with the pay of ensign). [136] He is again mentioned in September 1777. "Capt. Benjamin Hine was appointed to take the command at the fort at Milford in the rank and pay of a lieutenant and to enlist six men in addition to the number then on duty there; to continue in service until the 1st day of January, 1778; to keep up necessary guards and supply the men in the fortification as constant as might be." [137]

Lastly, in the Session of February 5, 1778: "Benjamin Hine was appointed a Lieutenant of a company of artillery men to be stationed at Milford." [138]

Middlebury Cemetery records reveal that his tombstone reads: Hine, Capt. Benjamin d. Nov. 8, 1800 aged 81 years. (in the 82nd year of his age) [139]

Church records simply note: "Vet. Rev. War [140]

ENOS BENHAM   1745 – 19 Jun 1811

Benham is: "Listed under Capt. Nathaniel Edwards Co. of Gen. David Waterbury's State Brigade. [He] joined Apr. 2, 1781 at Wallingford. In March 1781, Brig. Gen. Waterbury Jr. was appointed Commandant of the Battalion to be raised for the defense of the post at Horseneck [named for a horse pasture in Greenwich] and places adjacent, and also all the guards raised for the defense of the Seacoasts from Horseneck to New Haven inclusive. The force was composed of drafts from the Militia and amounted to a brigade of two battalions. In July it joined Washington while he was en-camped at Phillipsburg and for some time after was under Heath's orders on the Westchester line. Col. Meigs lately returned from the Conn. Line was first assigned this command but he declined the service" [141]

136 RRH, p. 391.
137 Ibid. p. 491.
138 Ibid. p. 520.
139 PRD, p. 316.
140 SMB, p. H-9.
141 HPJ, p. 567.

Johnson also reveals that, earlier in the war, Benham served as " Fifer in Capt. James Peck's Co. of Col. Roger Enos' Battalion State Regiment as of Sep. 17, 1777." [142]

The census of 1810, p. 666, shows Benham's ID number as CT3603997, while Church records list Benham as: "Vet. Rev. War Capt. James Peck's Co. Col. Roger Enos' Battalion – 1777 [143]

DANIEL CLARK   1763 – 29 Aug 1847

Little is known of Daniel Clark except that he is listed in the: "Census of Pensioners in 1840." Middlebury Church records confirm this, listing him as: "Vet. Rev. War Pensioner 1840." [144]

Anderson tells us that he was the son of Thomas Clark and married Hannah Nichols of Lebanon, in October of 1772.

His burial Inscription reads: died Aug 29, 1847, aged 84. Abigail Northrop, wife of Daniel Clark, died Feb. 25, 1835, age 69.

EZEKIAL TUTTLE   5 Jan 1718 – 6 Feb 1799

Originally from Woodbury, Tuttle is listed as a member of the Connecticut Line, 1777 – 81.

He served with the 4th Co. of Col. Douglas' regiment of the Connecticut militia and may have seen action in military actions along Lake George and Lake Champlain.

Cemetery records indicate: "d. Feb. 6, 1799, aged 82 yrs. [145]

Church records list him as: "Vet. Rev. War Ct. Line, 1777- 1781, Supplies 1777-1779."

SAMUEL TUTTLE   22 Feb 1743 – 1824

Samuel, son of Ezekial, above, served in Capt. Lewis' 4th Company of William Douglas' 5th Battalion of the Continental Line, after Douglas was promoted to Colonel. Douglas was taken back by how ill equipped the men had been. In the defeat at the Battle of Brooklyn, this company was in one of the last boats during the retreat to Manhattan. In the Battle of Kip's Bay, which soon followed, those same men fled panic-stricken and moved General Washington to remark, "Are these the men with whom I am to defend America?" He allegedly struck some of them with the blade side of his sword, to encourage them to fight.

---

142 Ibid. p. 615.
143 SMB. P. B-15.
144 SMB, p. C-
145 PRD, p. 318.

He died in Windham, New York in 1824

CAPT. ISAAC BRONSON   **2 OCT 1736 – 15 Apr 1826**

Isaac Bronson was the great grandson of Isaac the Planter. He served as Captain in Col. Sheldon's Light Dragoons, beginning in 1777. Custom has it that this Isaac Bronson may have entertained General Washington while he was en route to a meeting with Le Comte de Rochambeau, in September of 1780, or possibly in May of 1781, when the General met Rochambeau in Wethersfield to discuss plans for the latter to join Washington's army at Peekskill, New York. More on this later.

Church records list Bronson as: "Capt. Vet Rev War [146] Col. Elisha Sheldon's Light Dragoons, 1777-1783. Some may have attributed this record to his son. But Dr. Isaac removed to Greenfield Hill, and died there in 1838. Although unlikely, it appears that father and son both served under the same command. See page 36 and below.

DR. ISAAC BRONSON   **10 Mar 1760 – 19 May 1839**

Dr. Isaac Bronson, son of Capt. Isaac and great great grandson of Isaac, the Planter, pursued the study of medicine with Dr. Lemuel Hopkins of Hartford and entered the army as a junior surgeon. Like his father before him, he was assigned to the 2nd Regiment of Light Dragoons on 14 Nov 1779, in the Continental Line, under Col. Elisha Sheldon (of Salisbury) and in the direct command of General Washington. [147] He served on the "East side of Hudson along Westchester front, Maj. Benj. Talmadge of Wethersfield. Wintered generally in Conn. In '80-'81 – sent to Western Mass. Where hay and forage were plenty. Regt. disbanded June, '83." [148]

ASAHEL BRONSON   **28 Nov 1759 – 23 Apr 1850**

Asahel was the son of James Bronson and a cousin of Isaac IV, above. He "Signed on, on Apr. 1, 1777 for 1 month, 19 days. Conn Militia. Capt. Samuel Camp's Co. [6th Company] of Col. Noadiah Hooker's (of Farmington) [2nd] Regt. under Brig. Gen. Erastus Wolcott. At Peekskill Mar – Jun 1777. White Plains, Crampond, Fishkill, Ft. Montgomery, etc. Body of militia to serve for 6 weeks at Peekskill where Gen. McDougall was posted with a few troops." [149]

---

146 SMB, p. B-52.
147 BRH, p. 370-74.
148 HPJ, p. 271.
149 Ibid. p. 501.

He is also listed in the Census of Pensioners in 1840. [150]

Church records indicate that he was a: "Farmer, b. in Waterbury – d. Apr 23, 1850– age 90 yrs. Adm. (church rec.) Nov 9, 1817 Vet Rev War Pensioner 1840. Buried 1850. [151]

MICHAEL BRONSON   24 Mar 1754 – 1839

Michael was born to Ezra and Susanna Judd Bronson on the 24th of March, 1754. Hinman lists him as serving as 2nd Lieutenant in the 6th company under Capt. John Lewis, in the 5th battalion led by Col. William Douglas in 1776. The General Assembly on 14 June of that year ordered: "six Battalions to be raised and march directly to New York to join the continental army." [152] The 5th battalion, under Douglas, whose 4th company was composed of Waterbury men. It was stationed at Kip's Bay in New York, near Thirty-fourth Street. The British ships ascended the North (Hudson) and East Rivers to trap Washington's army after it was evacuated from Brooklyn and the defeat there. The great general was frustrated until this company, together with Col. John Glover's 14th Continentals were able to hold off the British long enough for Washington's army to flee across the King's Bridge and escape entrapment on Manhattan island.

MICHAEL BOWERS   1758 – 30 Aug 1840

Again, little is known of Bowers except that Johnson lists him on the: "List of Pensioners residing in New Haven County, 1832. [153]

Church records indicate that he was "adm. Sep 10, 1815 from Second Church, Milford d. 30 Aug 1840. M. Electa Manville of Middlebury, May 7, 1827 by Rev Mark Mead. [154]

His burial Inscription reads: "died Aug 30, 1840, aged 82. Verse: ......
through all Eternity."

STEPHEN HAWLEY   1767 – 5 Aug 1818

Hawley was one of the earliest physicians in town. According to Johnson, he served in the: 8th Co., 5th Regt. May 15-Oct 13, 1775. This was Gen. David Wooster's Continental Regiment. Col. David Waterbury (of Stanford), Capt. Jos. Smith (of Newtown). [155]

---

150 Ibid. p. 661.
151 SMB, p. B-44.
152 RRH, p. 227.
153 HPJ, p. 645.
154 SMB, p. B-30.
155 HPJ, p. 69. Ap.

Delia Bronson tells us: "Dr. Stephen S. Hawley located one mile east of the center before 1800; this was the opposite side of the road from Lift-the-Latch Inn on land now (1930) owned by the Joseph Regan estate. The cellar and well are still visible." [156] A pump station was (2010) constructed on that site. We know little of his medical practice, within the bounds of the present Middlebury.

His tombstone in the present cemetery reads: "Doct. Stephen S., d. Aug 5, 1818, aged 51 yrs. [157] Adjacent to the graves of Dr. Hawley and his wife, Dorcas, are at least eight tiny stones, indicating the burial sites of small children. A daughter lived to the age of sixteen. Tragically, for someone who dedicated his life to helping others, only one daughter would survive him.

Church records list Dr. Hawley as: "Vet Rev War – Continental Regt. 1775 d. Aug 5, 1818, age 51 yrs. Funeral Aug 7, 1818 [158]

DAVID PORTER   11 May 1746 – 1 Apr 1826

Porter was a descendant of Dr. Daniel Porter, an original settler near Hop Swamp. He was the son of James Porter and Dorcas Hopkins and married Esther Hopkins in 1775, before setting out upon his military service. [159] He served in "Capt. Heicock's Co. [as an] Ensign. [He]Arrived in camp Aug 16, discharged Sep 10, 1776. [and was a part of the]13th Regiment of Militia. [under] Col. Benjamin Hinman of Woodbury, commanding. Campaign Around New York, 1776. [He was]Called up in summer of '76 When Washington was in need of a large force to meet a threatened attack of the enemy upon New York. Brig. Gen. Oliver Wolcott. 14 regiments lying west of the Conn. River called out in August. Troops hastily summoned, poorly armed and provided for, and generally undisciplined." [160]

Delia Bronson indicated: "David Porter lived in the old house built probably about where Antonio Ferrante now (1930) lives." [161] This was located just off the Southford Road near its junction with Christian road.

---

156 BRD, p. 8.
157 PRD, p. 316.
158 SMB, p. H-5.
159 AND, p. 105 ap.
160 HPJ, p. 467.
161 BRD, p. 4.

Grave markings indicate: (In Memory of Mr. David Porter who) died April 1, 1826 Age 80. [162] Church records state: "Vet Rev War - Dayton Robbery – d. Apr 14, 1826 age 80. Buried 1826." [163]

JAMES PORTER   19 Nov 1737 – 10 NOV 1822

James Jr., an older brother of David, served in: Gen. David Waterbury's State Brigade. [164] [He] Joined Apr. 23, 1781. [and served at] Horseneck and surrounds. [165] He also served as: Ensign from Waterbury. [in]Col. Samuel Canfield's (of New Milford) Militia Reg't. [He was]At West Point, 1781 [under] Maj. Hazekiah Huntington. [166] He married Lucy Bronson, in November of 1762. [167] She was the daughter of Lt. Josiah of Breakneck and his first wife, Diana Sutliff, who died in childbirth. Middlebury Church records indicate that he rose to the rank of: "Capt. Vet Rev War d. Nov 22, 1822, age 85 Funeral Nov 12, 1822." [168]

DAVID ABBOTT   1764 – 7 NOV 1826

Delia Bronson's history relates "David Abbott, son of Daniel, married Sarah Tyler, daughter of James and sister of the Reverend Bennett Tyler, in 1786. He must have built the house where Mrs. Foote's house now stands. [Corner of Breakneck Hill and Watertown Roads] Of their twelve children, seven settled within a mile of the old place, so that, a century ago, there were forty-seven of the name Abbott here, only one remaining at the present time. [1930]" [169]

Johnson reveals that Abbott served in: 5th Batt. Wadsworth's Company, Conn. State Troops, Col. William Douglas (of Northford) 1776. Armorer: appointed Jul. 3, Discharged Nov. 3, 1776. [170]

Church records read: "d. Nov 7, 1826, age 62 Funeral Nov 9, 1826" [171]

---

162 PRD, p. 317.

163 SMB, p. P-10.

164 See also, Gedeon Platt and Enos Benham.

165 HPJ, p. 565.

166 Ibid. p. 582.

167 AND, p. 105 app.

168 SMB, p. P-12.

169 BRD, p. 5.

170 HPJ, p. 406.

171 SMB, p. A-2.

AARON BENEDICT   17 JAN 1745 – 16 DEC 1841

Benedict was: "born 17 Jan 1745 in Danbury. Conn. Removed to Waterbury the same year and settled in the east part of what is now the town of Middlebury; became a leading man in the town; was active in the Revolutionary War [Militia. North River [the Hudson] at Fishkill, N.Y. and Battle of Quebec.] Died 16 Dec 1841 age 97." [172]

Delia Bronson adds: "[1771] Aaron Benedict came from Danbury, bought land from Mr. [John] Thompson and helped him finish the house. Later Mr. Benedict built his house on the corner of Park Road and Straits Turnpike. This house was burned March 26th, 1916." [173]

Johnson tells us more specifically of his military service that he was a: "Sargent in Lieut. Isaac Benham's (of Waterbury) command. 10th Regt. of Militia. Was at New York 1776. [174]

Later, he too was made a: "Lieutenant at 9 £. Paid. Lt. Col. J. Baldwin's Regt. Paid as Bounty at Fishkill in the month of Oct. 1777 by Lt. Col. From State of Conn. Which had been ordered to march to the aid of the Continental Army on the North River. [the Hudson] [175]

He is also listed on the: "Census list of pensioners in 1840 at ae. 95," [176] while church records list Benedict as: "Vet Rev War Pensioner 1840. d. Dec 16. 1841 – ae. 97 (Church Rec.) Adm. My 15, 1803" [177]

CAPT. SAMUEL FENN   1746 – 13 MAR 1852

Fenn's military history indicates that he was a: "Sergeant, Lt. Col. J Baldwin's Regt. [see above] Capt. Jehiel Bryant's Co., Col. Joseph Thomson's Regt. of Militia ordered to march from Connecticut to aid the Continental Army at Peekskill in October of 1777. Marched from Oct. 5 – discharged Oct. 26." [178]

He apparently rose to the rank of Captain, as indicated on his tombstone.

ANDREW S. CLARK   1752 – 18 OCT 1835

Records indicate that Andrew served in "Lt. Clark's Co. in Col. J. Douglas's Regt. 21st Regt. of Militia. He entered Sep 1, discharged Nov

172 BRH, p. 465.
173 BRD, p. 5.
174 HPJ, p. 460.
175 Ibid. p. 522.
176 Ibid. 661.
177 SMB, p. B-13.
178 HPJ, p. 523.

10 at New York, 1776. [179] Prior to this service, he was a member of Maj. John Skinner's Light Horse, June 10 to Aug. 3, 1776. [180] And later he would be assigned to Capt. Jubez Fitch's Co. of Independent Volunteers. March 12 1782 – Jan 12, 1783, a part of Col. Samuel Caulfield's Regt. at West Point. [181] His name appears on the List of Pensioners of 1832 in New Haven County. [182] The Records of the Middlebury church indicate that Clark was: "Adm. Nov 10, 1811 from Milford, First Society." And he "d. Oct 18, 1835 ae. 83 yrs. Vet Rev War Pensioner 1832." [183]

JOHN THOMPSON   1746 – 24 APR 1801

Delia Bronson tells us: "John Thompson of Stratford was the first settler on Mount Fair, building a log house. About two years later he built the house now standing." (1930), while Johnson lists him as "Private, 8th Regiment Connecticut Line [see Aaron Benedict] Col. John Chandler's (of Newington) Reg't. Capt. Stoddard's Co. Signed on May 15, 1777 for three-year term. Killed by round shot from one of enemy's ships at defense of Fort Mifflin on the Right bank of the Delaware, Mud Island, Pa. Nov. 15, 1777. April 14, 1777 Chandler's Reg't. ordered to rendezvous at Danbury. While the Reg'ts. Were going into camp, the enemy under Tryon attempted their expedition against Danbury. Was encamped at Peekskill by middle of July. After American defeat at Brandywine Sept. 11, 1777, Washington directed Gen. Putnam to send reinforcements. Col. Chandler's Reg't. together with three others, assigned to Gen. MacDougall and participated in the Battle of Germantown, Pa. Oct. 4[th.] During retreat, twenty-two in regiment killed or injured. Washington, soon after, withdrew to Valley Forge. [184]

SAMUEL BENHAM   1737 – 12 Mar, 1823

Johnson indicates that Benham served in the "1st Reg't. Colonel David Wooster's (of New Haven), 7th Co. under Capt. Isaac Cook Jr. of Wallingford." He was "discharged in the North department 28 Nov 1775." [185]

179 HPJ, p. 474.
180 Ibid. p. 476.
181 Ibid. p. 584.
182 Ibid. p. 657.
183 SMB, C-8.
184 HPJ, p. 238.
185 Ibid. p. 42.

He also reveals that he served in the "6th Co. under Capt Jacob Brackett of New Haven. Fifth Batt. of Wadsworth's Brigade, under Col. William Douglas of Northfield." [186]

Benham then served with the "Minute Men and Volunteers, 1776. Drummer, with Enos Benham, fifer, in Capt. James Peck's Co. Col. Enos' State Reg't. Sept 17, 1777." [187]

Church records indicate that he lived to a ripe old age: "Benham, Mr. Samuel – Fnrl. May 13, 1823 aged 86 yrs." [188]

EDWARD BLACKMAN   1755 – 18 Dec 1827

Johnson tells us that on 10 July to 10 Oct. 1775, Blackman served with the 9th Co. under Capt. Peter Burrett (of Milford) in the 9th Regt. under Col. Charles Webb (of Stamford)

By order of Gen. Assembly July 1775, they were stationed at various points along the Sound until Sept 14, when on requisition from Washington, the Reg't. was ordered to the Boston Camp.

He was assigned to Gen. Sullivan's Brigade on Winter Hill at the Left of the besieged line and remained until expiration of Service, 31 Dec 1775 [189]

Church records indicate: d. Dec 18, 1827, Fnrl. Dec. 19, 1827, aged 72 yrs. [190]

ELIJAH BRONSON   May 15, 1755 –

Delia Bronson's history tells us that Elijah Bronson was the "son of Josiah [Lieut.] lived in the old house below Irving Baldwin's [junction of Breakneck Hill and Mirey Dam Roads] as did his son, Silas.

Anderson confirms this fact: "Elijah Bronson, son of Lieut. Josiah, m. Lois Bunnell d. of Stephen of Wallingford, Mar. 10, 1778" [191]

Church records of Elijah read: Orig. mem. Feb. 10. 1796 dis. to Otisco, N.Y. Oct. 11, 1818 [192]

Rev. Beauchamp of Onondaga Co., New York tells us of Bronson's service: "The name appears in Hartford Co. CT in 1796, and again in Col. [P.B.]Bradley's Reg't., serving in New York, where he was made a prisoner,

---

186 Ibid. p. 408.
187 Ibid. 615.
188 SMB, p. B-20.
189 HPJ, p. 52.
190 SMB, B-24.
191 AND, p. 26-ap
192 SMB, p. B-47.

being released Dec. 26, 1776. The name was unusual and was in Capt. Beebe's Co. in '76." [193]

BENJAMIN FENN   1757 – 11 Dec. 1854
Henry Johnson lists Fenn as a: "Private in Capt. Peck's Co. 3rd – Conn. State Troops, 1776. 5th Battalion of Wadsworth's Brigade. 4th Co. under John Lewis of Waterbury was in this (?) battle as well." [194]

He also lists him in the: "2nd Reg't. of Militia Companies from New Haven, Milford, Branford and Derby. Lt. Col. Appointed Oct 1776 – resigned 1777." [195]

Burpee clarifies this further: "A Waterbury company in Thadeus Cook's 2nd Battalion of Volunteers was raised in November, 1776 to serve until Mar 15, 1777." This company also included Isaac Bronson as 1st Lieutenant and Benjamin Fenn Jr. as Ensign. [196]

Anderson simply indicates: "Listed as 'Ens. Benjamin Fenn, Jr." on list of Rev. Soldiers" [197]

He is also on the "List of Pensioners New Haven Co. 1832" [198] and again on the "List of Pensioners of 1840 at age 84." [199]

Middlebury church records show that Fenn lived a long life here: "Adm. May 18, 1800 d. Dec. 11, 1854 age 97." [200]

ISRAEL FRISBIE
Johnson lists Israel Frisbie as being a "Sergeant in Capt. Samuel Camp's Co. of Militia." He indicates that the company "Marched April 1 for 1 month, 19 days in 1777." Camp's company was part of "Col. Hooker's (of Farmington) Regiment; Brig. Gen. Erastus Wolcott's (of Windsor) Brigade." He also tells us that the company was "At Peekskill, March to June, 1777. Continental Line of Militia – 3 Regts. Baldwin's, Hooker's and Moseley's sent to aid Gen. MacDougall. White Plains, Crampond, Fishkill, Ft.Montgomery,etc. [201]

193 WMB, p. 252.
194 HPJ, p. 408.
195 Ibid. p. 432.
196 CWB, p. 16.
197 AND, p. 462.
198 CNP, p. 654.
199 Ibid. p. 661.
200 SMB, p. F-2.
201 HPJ, p. 501.

Anderson tells us only that Frisbie came from Branford and married Active Foot on 22 Sep 1783." [202] He adds later that Active died in August, 1791, at age 28, not long after giving birth to a son, Israel Jr., on July 20th, no doubt from childbed fever. [203]

REUBEN HICKOX

Little is known of Hickox other than the fact that Johnson states he: "Enlisted Apr. 29, 1777 for 1 month, 22 days. Probably served with Israel Frisbie. [204] He is buried in the Middlebury Cemetery.

TIMOTHY HIGGINS

Johnson tells us that Higgins: "Served in Brig. Gen. Erastus Cook's Brigade, Col. Thomas Baldwin's Regt. and under Capt. Jared Shepherd, Mar. 30 - May 19, 1777." [205] Later that year he was "Under Brig. Gen. John Sullivan, Capt. Jehiel Bryant, Marched Oct. 5th – Disch. Oct. 15th." [206]

More specifically, Higgins was in "Col. Joseph Thompson's Regt. ordered to march from Ct." They were sent "To aid the Continental Army at Peekskill, October, 1777." [207]

JUSTUS JOHNSON

Henry Johnson records that Justus served in "Capt. Edward Rogers' Co. (from Cornwall) 3rd Co. 2nd Batt.Wadsworth's Brigade. His Ensign was Joel Hinman, from Woodbury." [208] Further along, he tells us he was in "Capt. Heacock's Co. 13th Regt., [under Col. Benjamin Hinman] Connecticut Militia. At N.Y. 1776." [209]

JOHNATHAN SANFORD

One of the very few Middlebury men to have deserted his service before his enlistment was up; Sanford served in "Col. Joseph Thompson's Co. Lt. Col. Baldwin's Regt. Connecticut Militia, 1777. Lt. Aaron Benedict, Capt. Jehiel Bryant's Co. October 5th to 15th - DESERTED. Company was ordered to march from Ct. to aid the Continental Army at Peekskill

202 AND, p. 53 app.
203 Ibid. p. 163 app.
204 HPJ, p. 501.
205 Ibid. p. 249.
206 Ibid. p. 523.
207 Ibid. p. 567.
208 Ibid. p. 397.
209 Ibid. p. 467.

in October of 1777." [210] Desertion was not unusual in those early days of the war.

BENJAMIN BEMONT (BEMENT)   1755 -
Bemont is listed in the Census of 1810, p. 669. # CT3603879. He is also "Listed as Pensioner in 1840 under Wolcott at age 85." [211]Anderson lists him amongst the revolutionary soldiers serving during the war. [212]

Delia Bronson records that: "Benjamin Bement settled southwest of Hop Swamp between John and Timothy Porter's probably near where Mrs. Henry Bowers lives, for he is described as having land in Mashaddock." [213]

Anderson places him on his list of soldiers serving in the Revolutionary War. [214]

TITUS BRONSON   15 Oct 1751 – 26 May 1820
Following upon the skirmishes at Lexington and Concord on April 19, 1775, the Connecticut legislature was swift to pass an act for enlisting and equipping one fourth of the state's standing militia, "for the safety and defense of the colony." They were to be divided into six regiments, and the companies to contain 100 men each. The Eighth Company of the 1st Regiment was raised in Waterbury and commanded by Major General David Wooster. Isaac Bronson III was a First Lieutenant in this Company. Their term of service was not to exceed seven months. The Company served in Fairfield County in defense of the seacoast towns then marched to the Hudson River then north towards Albany and Lake Champlain. The terms of the men expired while there but some chose to remain and were with Generals Montgomery and Wooster at the taking of Montreal. [215]

*****

In March of 1776, Boston was evacuated by the British army, in deference to New York and Congress requested of Connecticut more troops. The Legislature then responded by the raising, through voluntary enlistment this time, of seven regiments to join the Continental Army in

210 Ibid. p. 523.
211 CNP, p. 661.
212 AND, p. 461.
213 BRD, p. 4.
214 AND, p. 461.
215 BRH, p. 336-37.

New York. The Sixth Company of the Fifth Regiment was from Waterbury under Capt. John Lewis, Jr. In August 1776, after the Declaration of Independency and at the request of General Washington, all militia west of the Connecticut River were ordered to New York "until the present exigency is over." [216] By November, the General Assembly established four battalions (Regiments) The 2nd Battalion, commanded by Col Thaddeus Cook, included one Company from Waterbury, in which Isaac Bronson Jr. was serving as its First Lieutenant and Benjamin Fenn, Jr. as Ensign. [217]

Towards the end of 1776, the Legislature re-organized the state's militia companies into six brigades. The third Company from Waterbury now had Isaac Bronson Jr. as its Captain and Aaron Benedict as its Lieutenant. [218] No sooner had this change occurred than the Legislature re-organized once again, in accordance with a resolution from Congress. This time eight battalions were raised through volunteer enlistment and many serve to the end of the war. [219]

In April 1777, General Tryon and the British Army invaded Connecticut for the first time. They focused on Danbury where military stores were located and the town burnt. In response, many of the neighboring militia companies came to take part in the action. General Wooster was mortally wounded. Later, Col. Baldwin was stationed with his regiment at Fishkill and on the Hudson in New York, preventing communication between General Burgoyne, coming down from the north, and the British army at New York. [220]

In October of 1777, the Assembly ordered that the various companies be supplied with clothing and bullets. The town of Waterbury responded generously, including the families living in West Farms. In that same month, Gen. Burgoyne was captured and some West Farms men were a part of Gen. Gates' army of the north at the time. In 1778, the companies of Waterbury were formed into a distinct regiment, the 28th. [221]

In response to an engagement with a portion of the British army at Horseneck landing (West Greenwich) here in Connecticut, in December of 1780, Waterbury once again mustered a number of militia to aid in the

216 Ibid. p. 338.
217 Ibid. p. 339.
218 Ibid. p. 340.
219 Ibid.
220 Ibid. p. 343.
221 Ibid. p. 345.

defense of that area in early 1781. West Farms also responded with supplies, livestock and what little ammunition it could spare.

No person from the west farms section of Waterbury rose above the rank of Major, during the war of revolution. But Isaac Bronson III served the war effort as a Captain, while Aaron Benedict served as Lieutenant.

Chapter VIII

The War gets Personal for Some

With the evacuation of Boston by the British, in March of 1776, the Continental Army moved its primary theatre of operations from that town, in deference to the enemy's approaching New York. This meant that many of the troops traveled along the main inland route from Hartford, through Farmington, Southington and Waterbury. Their route coursed through Breakneck, on its way towards Fishkill, New York. Some of those troops would have a lasting impression on one little girl of that area.

Nathaniel Richardson, one of the early settlers upon Breakneck was born April 8, 1729, the fifth child of Ebinezer and Margit Warner Richardson. He lived high on the crest of Three Mile Hill, on Colonial Avenue – then known as the woodbury road. This house sits on the corner of what is now Acme Drive. He and his wife, Phoebe Bronson, daughter of John and Hannah Bronson, had their own daughter named Tamer. (or Tamar) who was born on Sept. 13, 1758. Nathaniel and Phoebe would have eight children in that house, which was built in 1760.

Dr. Anderson chronicles Tamer's experiences during the war of Revolution. In quoting her granddaughter, Mrs. Gilbert Hotchkiss of Waterbury, he writes:

"Many times has my grandmother told me of the soldiers of the Revolution passing her father's house [located on the woodbury road] [222] on the way to and from Boston and Fishkill stopping there for provisions or staying overnight, or both, and always keeping a guard. She told how

---

222 This house has been known at various times as the Richardson, Wallace, Curtis or Ruccio home.

she and her mother would bake all day as fast as they could, one oven-full after the other, the soldiers taking the pies as fast as they could bake them, and how her arms have been burned from the heat of the brick oven – and that with weary feet and aching limbs the only way to get to her room was to walk over the soldiers who lay thick upon the floor." [223] Except for the addition of the garage and modern amenities, the house in which she lived is preserved much in the way it had existed during the war of Revolution. The house still faces east, taking advantage of the view across Three Mile Hill. The old road, into what was once a sizeable farm, is still visible to the east side of this house as it passes in front of it.

Tamar Richardson later married Stephen Hotchkiss, also of Waterbury, in 1778 and lived to the ripe old age of 94. She was buried in the Grand Street Cemetery, the graves of which were dispossessed in 1890, in favor of a town park. Her tombstone is supposed to have read: "Tamar, wife of Stephen Hotchkiss, died Mar 29, 1853 AE 94 ½ Years."

Dr. Bronson alludes to one of the many troop movements along the old Woodbury road as follows: "Teams for carrying goods and supplies ran frequently and regularly to and from Fishkill [New York]. [224] In the fall of 1777, after the capture of "Gentleman Johnny" Burgoyne, [225] a detachment of the American Army with the enemies' splendid train of artillery passed over the road to the eastward." The road, to which he alludes, runs through Breakneck and over Kelly Road towards Waterbury.

Anderson tells us that "sick soldiers" had become such a burden to the people living along the "Continental road running east and west through Waterbury" (and hence through Breakneck) that in July, 1780, some selectmen petitioned the General Assembly for "the cost arising by soldiers when sick on the road to and from the army belonging to this State." [226] Josiah Bronson tended just such a "sick soldier" as early as 1778, in his home at Breakneck.

The possibility of a visit to Breakneck from General George Washington remains the subject of the tenth chapter and, given the importance of the route to the men of the Revolution, is highly probable.

However, West Farms contributed not only its share of men but also supplies to the cause of the American Revolution. Anderson tells

223 AND, p. 457.
224 BRH, p. 357.
225 "Gentleman Johnny" Burgoyne was the British General in charge of Fort Ticonderoga.
226 AND, p. 448.

us Michael Bronson: "pursued after some wagons to Breakneck," and "furnished 12 ½ pounds of lead, and bailed two pots," [227] while Aaron Benedict transported [wheat flour, salt pork, tents and provisions] "for the army" to West Point. [228]

---

227 Ibid. p. 449.
228 Ibid.

Chapter IX

Mister Adams is Unimpressed

John Adams and the remainder of the Massachusetts delegation to the Continental Congress, meeting at Philadelphia, made several trips there prior to 1777. They had utilized the customary route from Hartford through New Haven and along the Post Road to New York and the City of Brotherly Love beyond. However, by 1777 things had changed considerably. With the evacuation of Boston on March 17, 1776, the major theatre of operations had shifted to New York. Following the signing of a Declaration of Independency on July 2nd of that year, Congress had adjourned for the summer and fall. However, Adams was returned once more to Congress for the subsequent session. Other delegates to that second session included his cousin, Samuel Adams, together with Francis Dana of Boston and Elbridge Gerry of Marblehead. The work of the Congress was still unfinished. There is no evidence that these delegates passed through Break Neck but given the circumstances, it is quite likely. We do know that John Adams and his man, Fessenden, certainly did.

In a letter to his wife, dated January 17th (or 18th) 1777, John Adams writes of his journey through Waterbury and Woodbury. His party stopped for the night in Fish Kill, New York, where he settled in to write the letter to Abigail. [229] *"After a March like that of Hannibal over the Alps We arrived last night at this place..."* he penned from Fishkill. Avoiding the more southern route he had previously taken, because the British were by then patrolling Long Island Sound, Adams and his party no doubt passed

---

229 John Adams to Abigail Adams, Adams Papers, Electronic Archive, Massachusetts Historical Society, 17 Jan 1777.

through Breakneck upon the old Woodbury road. He was yet again en route from the North Parish of Braintree, later Quincy, to the Continental Congress, meeting in Philadelphia. He described his journey on horseback thus: *"We came from Hartford through Farmington, Southington, Waterbury, Woodbury, New Milford, New Fairfield, the Oblong &c. to Fish Kill. Of all the mountains I ever passed these are the worst – We found one Advantage however in the Cheapness of Travelling."*

Commenting on his passage through Connecticut, Adams wrote *"I don't find one half the Discontent, nor the Terror here that I left in the Massachusetts. People seem sanguine that they shall do something grand this Winter."* Perhaps, Adams' sentiments reflect the fact that the Revolution had not as yet touched the people of West Farms in any meaningful way. They had responded generously to a call for food and supplies, during the embargo of the port of Boston. Some Connecticut men responded to a request for military assistance from General Israel Putnam after the skirmish at Lexington and Concord.

There is, at present, no known evidence, available to this writer that John Adams ever actually stopped in the Breakneck area of West Farms. Adams described the weather as severe and his new horse as serving him quite well, rambling up the mountainous terrain without difficulty.

It is evident from his letter, however, that Adams found the fine qualities of hope and courage in the people along the route he had taken. But their expectations for "something grand this Winter" would not materialize for another four years, until the British surrender at Yorktowne, Virginia. Unless, of course, one considers the great American victory in re-taking Trenton, on Christmas day, after a formidable crossing of the ice-filled Delaware River. In the interim, West Farms would provide its share of fine young men to the cause of freedom and serve as a stopping point for weary American troops and a model French army, enlisted to assist in the final victory.

This letter of John Adams addressed to his wife describes his travels through Breakneck on Jan. 17, 1777. (courtesy of Massachusetts Historical Society, Electronic Archives)

Adams actually made several trips along the route through Middlebury during his time in Congress and again as Vice President under George Washington. It is highly likely that he passed this way as President, as well. Although there are no other direct references to this area, as in the January, 1777 letter to his wife, he refers to the town of Brookfield, to the west of Breakneck, in his diary and in several additional letters. The middle post road carried Adams from Springfield, through Hartford, Waterbury, Southbury, Newtown and Brookfield, on any number of further occasions.

But it was not only John who passed this way. His wife, Abigail Adams, as first lady of the land, wrote John from Brookfield on Sunday, October 13, 1799. She was en route to Philadelphia, after a stop in East Chester to visit her daughter, Nabby, and family. Abigail penned: "Here I am at this favorite spot." And she goes on to say that she was "put up at Capt. Draper's. [230] She had some problems with one of her carriage horses, named Farmer: "so crippled is the poor animal that I know not how I shall get on with him, as he goes like a man with the goute." One wonders if the trip over the rugged hills of Breakneck may have contributed to her horse's indisposal. As we shall see in subsequent chapters, it was not only the Adamses who made their way up the challenging roads of this area of West Farms.

---

230 Ibid. 13 Oct 1799.

Chapter X

A French Connection and...

A Visit from His Excellency

At least once if not more during the War of Revolution, Général La Fayette, Gilbert du Motier, also passed this way. Dr. Bronson provides the details. The General, attended only by his aides, lodged at the house of Capt. Isaac Bronson, at Breakneck, who reportedly kept a tavern there. [231] It is true the captain did keep tavern here. The Grand List of August, 1872 confirms that the younger Bronson was assessed £20 as a tavern keeper. [232] In deference to his men, La Fayette chose to have the soft feather bed removed and replaced with the same straw upon which the common foot soldier slept. "Straw for the soldier," he reportedly said. [233] Bronson described the General as "a slender, handsome youth, who sat a horse beautifully, and altogether made a fine appearance." [234] He was only forty years old at the time.

In the summer of 1778, the Général was detached by Washington to assist in the expulsion of the British from Newport, Rhode Island. He would have once again passed through Breakneck from Fishkill, while en route there. However, the expedition failed miserably and in the fall, he no doubt returned by the same route, back to the Hudson to rejoin Washington's army encamped at Peekskill. [235]

---

231 BRH, p. 358.
232 AND, p. 486.
233 BRH, p. 358
234 Ibid.
235 Ibid.

His Excellency, General George Washington also passed through Connecticut on several occasions, between 1776 and 1781. It is reasonably established that the great man conferred with the Comte de Rochambeau in Hartford, from September 20th to the 22nd, 1780. Anderson notes that on September 17, 1780, "General Washington with the Marquis de la Fayette and General Knox with a splendid retinue left Tappan."[New York] The most direct route would have carried them through Breakneck. In March of 1781, Washington conferred with Rochambeau once again, on this occasion in Newport, Rhode Island. The two reviewed Lauzon's Hessian cavalry in Lebanon, Connecticut, where they were quartered. On a third occasion, May 21-30, 1781, they met in Wethersfield, no doubt to plan their strategy concerning the combined march to Yorktown, Virginia. [236]

Every town wants to take credit for "His Excellency" having rested, roomed or taken repast there. Middlebury is no exception. There is certainly enough circumstantial evidence to suggest such. Dr. Bronson also wrote that General Washington "passed through Waterbury, certainly once, on his way to Hartford." [237] He was alluding to the visit of September 1780. *"He rode a chestnut colored horse, came across Breakneck, and returned the salutations of the boys by the road side. His dignity of Manner, set off by his renown, made a durable impression on all who beheld him."* It is likely that the Comte de Rochambeau stayed with Capt. Isaac in the month of June 1781, en route to Yorktowne. This is discussed in a subsequent chapter.

The route over Breakneck, as previously noted, was part of the main east-west road, the so-called "middle post road," utilized for troop movements, primarily because it was the most southern route, still at a safe distance from the sea. [238] During this period, the Long Island Sound was clearly in the hands of the British. In the fall of 1777, after the capture of "Gentleman" Johnny Burgoyne at Saratoga, this road was utilized by a detachment of the American Army, to transport a portion of the enemy's "splendid train of artillery." Not all the captured weapons were hauled across Massachusetts, for use at Dorchester Heights. Some were floated down the Hudson, for use on other fronts.

On that occasion, the Americans camped at Manhan Meadows (just before the West Main Street bridge in the area of Colonial Plaza) in Waterbury. Hence, in addition to providing men and supplies, West Farms

236 Ibid. p. 359.
237 Ibid. p. 358
238 Ibid. p. 357.

found itself assisting the men of the Revolution in their troop movements on many an occasion.

But the road, which ran through West Farms, carried another enemy, from time to time, as American patriots moved in both directions. It carried pestilence as well. Any number of soldiers was ill with Small-poxe or "Camp fever" as they passed. Two such men, marching with Rochambeau's forces in 1781 had died before reaching the East Farms section of Waterbury and were buried there. A monument to these men was erected in the old East Farms cemetery off East Main Street in that town. They were en route from the camp [Camp 8] at Barnes's Tavern in Southington, to Breakneck. There is no evidence that any of the men died, while encamped here.

Chapter XI

The Comte de Rochambeau's Visit

Le Comte de Rochambeau was sent by the King of France, Louis XVI, 1780, at the head of the "Expedition Particuliere," which consisted of some 7000 foot soldiers and accompanying artillery. He landed in Newport, Rhode Island on July 10th but remained there for almost a year, because of his reluctance to abandon the French Fleet, which was blockaded in Narragansett Bay by the British. Born in Vendome, France, the Comte distinguished himself in the Seven Years War and was subsequently assigned the rank of Lieutenant General.

At last, on June 10 of 1781, Rochambeau and his men left Newport to join General Washington's army for the march south towards Yorktowne, Virginia. His route took him through the area known as Breakneck, in the West Farms of Waterbury, where his engineers had set up Camp 9.

> **"Here camped de Rochambeau.**
>
> **Out of the mystic long ago**
>
> **Tramp of feet And the trumpet's sound**
>
> **Robbed of my pomp and my war time show**
>
> **Grenadiers of mine ancient ground—**
>
> **Back to my rock bound broad plateau**
>
> **Where the fern and the nodding daisies grow.**
>
> **Back I come—de Rochambeau!"**

So wrote a recent Cornell University graduate by the name of Roland F. Andrews of Hartford, in 1904, for the dedication of a simple monument, commemorating that Encampment of the Comte de Rochambeau and his troops upon the hill called Breakneck, in what is now Middlebury. [239] The placing of the monument is attributed, by Delia Bronson, to Waterbury's Irish-American Club but she thought the reason for the Club's involvement was not clear. [240] Perhaps, she considered, it may be related to the fact that the Property upon which it stands, just west of the intersection of Artillery Road and Breakneck Hill, was owned by a Waterbury Irishman, named James F. Gaffney and sold, in 1904, to Dennis H. Tierney also of Waterbury. He, in turn, gifted that small tract where the monument rests, to the Town. Conveyance of the tiny plot, just six by six feet, was given with the understanding that it would forever be used to commemorate Rochambeau's encampment.

The Tierney deed is interesting, in that it tells us something of the physical features of the area. The land upon which the Rochambeau Monument is located was known, at least in 1904, as "the Orchard." The north side of the plot rested upon what was once an "old highway," which is clearly shown on the Beers' Atlas map of Middlebury (Plate 5 dated 1856,) a copy of which is owned by the author. The plot was bounded on the south and east by the property of James F. Gaffney, while on the west it abutted property of Mary A. Tyler. [241]

---

239 BRD, p. 43.
240 Ibid, p. 42.
241 Ibid. p. 43.

This Monument commemorating the Comte de Rochambeau's Camp 9 in Middlebury is located above the junction of Artillery and Breakneck Hill Roads (R. Sullivan photo)

William J. Pape, in his "History of Waterbury and the Naugatuck Valley, Connecticut" written in 1918, tells us that Mr. Tierney "devoted much of his time to securing belated recognition for the men of Rochambeau's army..." [242] He was responsible for the erection of monuments, mostly at his own expense, not only in Middlebury but at Fort Hill in Marion [Southington] and at the East Farms Cemetery in Waterbury, as well. Pape writes that Tierney, who died on June 11, 1916, "in 1902 erected a commemorative shaft [monument] at his own expense" at Breakneck Hill, Middlebury. [243] Pape may have been mistaken regarding the date, in his volume, although it is certainly plausible that the monument could have been erected almost two years before its dedication. Tierney was the vice president for Connecticut, not of Waterbury's "Irish- American Club" but of the American-Irish Historical Society, founded in Boston in 1897. It may have been his position in this society, which led to the Irish involvement in the erection of the Rochambeau monument. Or it

242 WJP. P. 317
243 Ibid.. P. 318.

may have been his interest in the presence of a Franco-Irish component in that Regiment of Rochambeau's army called the Volontaires-etrangers de Lauzon. In addition to a fair number of rank and file, Lauzon's second in command was also an Irishman named Robert Dillon.

Another mystery is the involvement of Roland F. Andrews of Hartford, in the writing of the dedicatory poem. Andrews graduated from Cornell University in 1900 and served on the Executive Board of the Connecticut Chapter of the Cornell Alumni Association. [244] He may have been associated with the American-Irish Historical Society or may have been solicited by Mr. Tierney to write the poem. It is even quite plausible that a contest may have been held for the honor.

*****

Not generally known is the fact that General Rochambeau camped in Middlebury, not once, but twice in the years 1781 and 1782. [245] Jean Baptiste Donatien de Viemeur, le Comte de Rochambeau, arrived in West Farms on June 27, 1781, after an exhausting thirteen mile march from the Barnes' (Baron's) Tavern, on "French Hill" in Southington, where he stayed the night previous. En route, he paused to bury two of his "soldats" at East Farms, who may have succumbed to camp fever. (Typhus) As noted above, Dennis H. Tierney of Waterbury was largely responsible for the erection of monuments at these sites.

244 See Cornell Alumni News, V. XVI, p. 421, May 28, 1914.
245 BRH, p. 359.

**Jean Baptiste Donatien de Viemeur, Le Comte de
Rochambeau (Courtesy of Ph. Evrard, pfef.)**

Perhaps the best source of information concerning Rochambeau's march through Connecticut comes from a member of the General's own staff: his Assistant Quartermaster General. Louis-Alexandre Berthier (1753-1815) was a Captain in the French Army when, on July 10, 1780, he was transported, by a rather circuitous route through the west indies, to join with 5400 officers and men (of these there were about 1000 support personnel) as an Expeditionary Force, or *expedition particulière,* in Newport, Rhode Island. The main body was carried to Newport by French Admiral d'Ternay and his fleet. Berthier served as "aide maréchal general des logis surnumeraire" in charge of logistics under the General and kept extensive maps and journals. This was quite natural a position for young Berthier, as his father was a prominent mapmaker to the French king, Louis XVI. It was young Berthier, who no doubt preceded Rochambeau to Breakneck, together with a contingent of French engineers, for the purpose of mapping the route and the area, where the French were to encamp. Fortunately for Middlebury residents, Berthier has provided us with the earliest known map of the Break Neck section of town and the main route from Waterbury to Woodbury.

The Force consisted of four divisions, each composed of roughly one fourth of the total contingent. The first division, referred to as the Regiment de Bourbonnis, was led by the comte de Rochambeau, under the command of Anne Alexandre marquis de Montmorency-Laval. Second in command of this division was Rochambeau's son, Donatien.

Antoine Charles du Houx baron De Vioménil, Rochambeau's second in command led the second division, the Regiment de Royal Deux Ponts. It was headed by Comte Christian de Forbach, while the third, the Regiment de Soissonais, was led by the Comte de Vioménil, the baron's son, and headed by the Comte de Sant Maisone. The fourth division consisted of the Regiment de Santonge, under the command of Adam Philippe Comte de Custine.

In addition to the above four divisions, each was accompanied by Artillery, under the overall command of Gerard d'Aboville. The Artillery included the Second Battalion of the Regiment d'artillerie d'Auxomme, under Goulett de La Tour. Another Regiment, the so-called Lauzon's Legion, composed of a multi-national force of volunteers, under Armand Louis Gontaut, Duc de Lauzon, was sent on ahead to protect Rochambeau's flank, to the south. The Legion never encamped in Middlebury.

Rochambeau's plan of organization was to send each division forward on four separate days, thus utilizing the same camps without overburdening them. The first division, with Rochambeau and his general staff in the lead, set out from Waterman's Tavern in Providence, Rhode Island, on June 18, 1781, for the march across Connecticut. They were to join Washington's forces at Philipsburg, New York (now Greensburgh). The Army had remained in Newport for almost a year, in order to support their Fleet, which was blockaded there by the British. The French fleet left Newport on June 11th of 1781 for Providence. The smartly dressed officers wore "coats of white broadcloth trimmed with green, white under-dress, and hats with two corners, instead of three..."Besides their muskets, the enlisted soldiers were burdened down with gaiters, wigs and tightly fitting woolen underwear and carried equipment weighing almost sixty pounds.

It must have been a most unusual and dramatic sight as the Regiment Bourbonnais, with Rochambeau mounted upon a fine steed at its head, marched two and two, up the Southington Mountain, through Waterbury, on the 27th day of June, 1781, to come at last, to Breakneck. Also following up the first division were the baggage train and the money chest. There were seven wagons of Rochambeau's luggage alone. The Artillery consisted of eight twelve-pounders and six mortars, divided up between the four divisions. A total of ten Regimental wagons accompanied each division, each drawn by a team of four horses. Needless to say, by the time they reached Breakneck, the army had to enlist all the local teams of oxen it could muster, in order to move the heavy artillery up the treacherous slope.

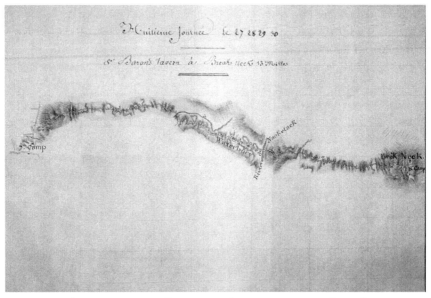

**The Route Map from Southington to Breakneck
drawn by Rochambeau's engineer Berthier, courtesy
of the Princeton University Archives.**

The French army had encamped in the Marion section of Southington the preceding night. Rochambeau had stayed at Barnes' Tavern there. But the march had taken its toll. By the time the army had struggled up the rugged terrain towards the East Farms of Waterbury, two French foot soldiers had died. They lie buried in the little known and quite hidden East Farms cemetery, just off East Main Street, where a simple stone marker commemorates their service to the budding new nation.

At Breakneck, the advance corps of engineers had prepared the area and set a camp. A beautifully drawn and water-colored map of the area is found in Captain Berthier's Journal IX. There is also a similarly beautiful and accurate color drawing of the route, which Rochambeau's army took from Southington.

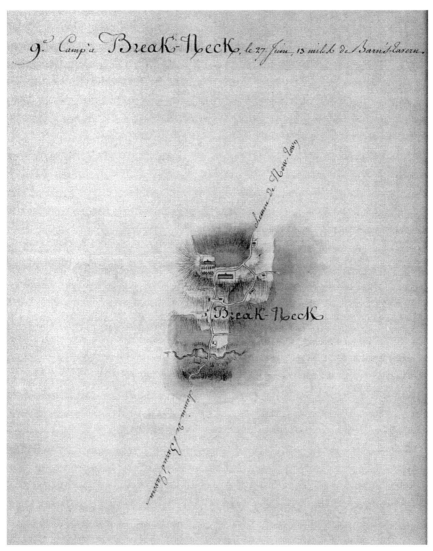

**Camp 9 at Breakneck, presently Middlebury,
Connecticut from the Berthier Collection, courtesy
of the Princeton University archives.**

General Rochambeau would have been entertained at Capt. Isaac Bronson's home, at the base of Breakneck and not at Lieut. Josiah's further up the hill. The captain's home was probably located in the vicinity of the James C. Tyler house but on the north side of Breakneck Hill Road.

The Journal of a young enlisted man, named Georg Daniel Flohr, assigned to the Royal Deux-Ponts regiment, chronicles his experiences upon Breakneck: "On the 29th [actually June 28th, 1781] we broke camp again and marched 13 miles to Break Neck, a little town in the mountains in a most beautiful area where the entertainments were even greater what with dancing and frolicking with the lovely beautiful American girls who lived there. All these entertainments took place in the open air." [246]

Flohr then wrote of breaking camp on the next morning and marching to Newtown, a distance of 13 miles to the west. He mentions passing through "a nice little hamlet called Gutbahr, about two English miles long. Dr. Bronson speculates that this may have referred to Southbury. In the author's opinion, Woodbury is more likely.

Contrast, however, the opinions of this enlisted man with the writings of some of Rochambeau's officers. "Five miles beyond the 'Waterbury River,'" writes Lieutenant Clermont-Crevecoeur, with the first division, "lay Breakneck, an assemblage of 'two or three houses.' The roads were 'detestables' and the first division reached Breakneck on June 27 only with 'the greatest difficulty...the village is frightful and without resources." [247]

Clermont-Crevecoeur wrote: "our horses could do no more so we had to commandeer all the oxen we passed and go far afield to find others in order to reach camp with our guns. We never had a worse day, considering the fatigues and misfortunes we endured." Bear in mind, however, that the enlisted men were clothed in light linen (although they had woolen underwear), while the officers endured the heavy woolen costume befitting their rank. Capt. Berthier described the area thus: "the village contains few houses. These are widely scattered and very ugly." However, he did leave the very beautiful drawings of the route to and from the camp at Breakneck, as aforementioned, which are now in the Princeton University Archives.

"On...the 28th, we were very weary before we got to Breakneck," wrote Baron von Closen, one of Rochambeau's aides-de-camp, "It is rightly named 'casse-col' [248] for the stony roads and the endless mountains intersecting

---

246 DRS, p. 42.
247 Ibid. p. 70.
248 French for "Break-neck"

the area make it very disagreeable for travelers. [249] It was not only the enlisted man who took advantage of his time on Breakneck to frolic and enjoy himself. Baron Closen remembered the "two very pretty young ladies whom we found in M. de Viomeuil's quarters (no doubt the Josiah Bronson House referred to above) [and who] seemed to have fallen from the clouds to receive us and console us a little for our fatigues of the day."

The Josiah Bronson House built in 1738, located on Breakneck Hill (from the Middlebury Historical Society collection)

---

249 BRD, p. 42.

The Bronson House as it has been restored by Lawrence Duryea (from the Middlebury Historical Society collection)

Another officer, the Comte de Lauberdiere, described two "beautiful maidens" as looking "very much like the Queen of France." Dr. Bronson suggests that one of these girls may well have been "Esther, the daughter of Josiah Bronson, who kept a tavern at the foot of Breakneck Hill, and who is reported to have locked her up for fear she would elope with a French officer." [250]

However, this may be more myth than fact, as Henry Bronson fails to list an "Esther" as an offspring of Josiah Bronson. Also, Josiah's house was not at the "foot of Breakneck Hill" but rather, half way up the eastern slope. Josiah did, however, have two daughters: Lucy, born Sep. 10, 1736, who married James Porter of this town and Zuba, born Apr. 28, 1745, who married Abner Munson but they were long gone from the household before the French arrived. Capt. Isaac, on the other hand, had several daughters and did live at the foot of the hill.

As Rochambeau and the first division departed on the following day for the next encampment (Number 10) in Newtown, the second division (Deux Ponts) arrived. The third (Soissonais) arrived on June 29th while

---

250 DRS, p. 28.

the fourth (Sant'Onge) under the Comte de Custine arrived on June 30th. Thus, the last of the French Expeditionary Force left Breakneck at West Farms on July 1st, 1781, heading north, then west on the present-day Breakneck Hill Road towards Woodbury.

This was not the last time the residents of West Farms were to see Rochambeau and his Army, however. What followed for the French contingent is generally quite well known, for, at Yorktown, Virginia, on October 19th of that memorable year, Cornwallis' British army surrendered to Generals Washington and Rochambeau, to end the War of Revolution.

William Cothren refers to "La Fayette's Army" as opposed to Rochambeau and suggests that in 1781 that army encamped in Woodbury, on their journey south to join General Washington. He describes how they "came through White Deer Rocks where they were obliged to cut away trees, and remove Stones in order to transport their heavy baggage through this defile." [251] No doubt mistakenly, and perhaps referring to an earlier visit by La Fayette himself, Cothren suggests that the Général stayed at "the house of Hon. Daniel Sherman and was waited on by all of the prominent men of the town." He goes on to suggest that the French Army encamped in tents, all along the main road through town, "from the Middle Quarter to White Oak, a distance of nearly three miles." [252] We know, however, from the writings of members of the French army itself, that in 1781 they had camped at Breakneck. We also know that La Fayette himself, during this time, was already with General Washington waiting for Rochambeau's forces to join them.

After wintering in the warmer climes and waiting for safer conduct, the French left their camps at Yorktown and Williamsburg, to head north in two divisions, on July 1, 1782. They entered Connecticut on October 23rd and on the 26th day of that month, arrived at Breakneck (Camp 42) for the second time. A manuscript letter from Deacon Leonard Bronson to Dr. Henry Bronson indicated that "they stopped over one day to wash, bake and etc. All the wells in the neighborhood were drawn dry, and the people far and near were employed, with their teams, to cart water from Hop Brook." [253]

It is also rumored that, upon the return visit, General Rochambeau may have stayed in the home of Lieutenant Josiah Bronson, rather than at his nephew's just down the hill. That house remains to this day, occupied

251 WMC, p. 213.
252 Ibid.
253 BRH, p. 359.

for many years by Mr. And Mrs. Lawrence Duryea and presently occupied by the Richard Seman family.

There exists some controversy as to the exact location where Rochambeau stayed, while at Breakneck. Myth and self-service prevail. Dr. Bronson suggests that he stayed at Capt. Isaac Bronson's house. As was said, this was located on the north side of lower Breakneck, just up from Tyler Crossing and in the area opposite the James C. Tyler house. It was here, Dr. Bronson, suggests, that General le Marquis de Lafayette also stayed, on at least one of his passages through Waterbury. "He, at one time, attended only by his aides, lodged at the house of Capt. Isaac Bronson, who there kept a tavern. The host introduced him to his best chamber, in which was his best bed. But Lafayette caused the feather bed to be removed saying 'straw for the soldier;' and made the straw under-bed his couch for the night." Dr. Bronson also speculates that it may have been in the summer of 1778, on one of his journeys to or from the Hudson to Rhode Island, when Lafayette snuggled down, in what was to become, in 1807, the Town of Middlebury.

Lieutenant Clermont-Crèvecoeur, who marched with the artillery of the first division, has summed up his feelings concerning the country and people of Connecticut. One can expect that his words rang true of the early settlers of Break Neck, just as well.

He wrote: "It is unquestionably the most fertile province in America, for its soil yields everything necessary to life. The pasture is so good here that the cattle are of truly excellent quality. The beef is exceptionally good. The poultry and game are exquisite. (It is) one of America's best provinces…This country has a very healthy and salubrious climate. We have seen old people here of both sexes who enjoy perfect health at a very advanced age. Their old age is gay and amiable and not at all burdened with the infirmities that are our lot in our declining years. The people of the province are very hard-working, but they do not labor to excess as our peasants do. They cultivate only for their physical needs. The sweat of their brow is not expended on satisfying the extravagant desires of the rich and luxury loving; they limit themselves to enjoying what is truly necessary. Foreigners are cordially welcomed by these good people. You find a whole family bustling about to make you happy. Such are the general characteristics of the people of Connecticut." This is the fine first impression that the people of Breakneck left upon our generous visitors from France.

Chapter XII

Pestilence at West Farms

One of the most dreaded diseases of the 17th and 18th centuries in America was the scourge known as the Small Poxe. Widespread disease was known variously as "the Poxe" or even "the Plague." A process called variolation (from whence the Latin name for Smallpox is derived) - the introduction of scabs from an infected individual, powdered and introduced through the nose of a healthy person - would result in a milder form of the disease. This first occurred in China many centuries before and was introduced to this country, interestingly enough, by African slaves. Later the practice consisted of the introduction of pus from a pustule on a pox victim through a scratch on the skin. This would convey permanent immunity, if indeed the patient survived, to the variolated or inoculated individual. The practice was not completely safe. King George III lost a son to inoculation and John Adams' son Charles almost died, when Abigail had the family inoculated while Adams was away serving in Congress. Adams himself had "taken the poxe," that is, he was inoculated by Dr. Zebdiel Boylston in 1764.

Inoculation had been employed with fairly good success to counter Small poxe in 1735 in Philadelphia and again in Charleston, South Carolina in 1738, when epidemic smallpox had appeared in those cities. Another major outbreak occurred in New England between 1775 and 1782. Due to troop movements and living in close quarters, the problem became especially evident amongst the men of the American and British armies.

Although the passing of Rochambeau and his forces in 1781 carried pestilence to the populace, there is no written evidence that Smallpox was an issue. One Dr. Charles Upson became the first physician in Waterbury to inoculate against the "Small poxe" in February of 1782. Anderson tells us that the patient was named Ezra Mallory. [254] Mallory took three weeks to recover from the inoculation – in essence, suffering from a milder form of the actual disease and was cared for by one Wait Hotchkiss. Following upon this case, the town gave, "during forty-eight days," permission to all males in the town over ten years of age, and to all persons living on the east and west Continental road (as the road running through Middlebury was referred) "to take the infection of small pox by way of inoculation." [255] It can be assumed that such inhabitants had a greater degree of exposure to the disease, because of the constant military traffic along the route. Even then, they recognized some of the sources of contagion.

A committee of fifteen was formed, Dr. Anderson writes, which included in its membership the Rev. Mark Leavenworth, whose duty it was "to give orders respecting the time when the infection should be taken, the house or homes where the patients should live, the tendance (attendants) the time of their cleansing and the time of their release from restrictions – and to take whatever precautions should be deemed expedient for preserving the inhabitants from taking the infection."

The disease was recurring in increasing frequency amongst transient soldiers and inhabitants as well. The date set for the last day of the year on which inoculation could be provided was established as March 20th. In the late seventeen hundreds, it was also recognized that the occurrence of the disease called Small poxe was most prevalent during the summer months and all but disappeared during the cold of winter.

In 1784, Dr. Abel Bronson, son of Josiah Bronson of Breakneck, petitioned the town for permission to name a place "healthy, convenient and secure" where he might build a house to receive patients for inoculation. Under appropriate restrictions, as established by the aforesaid committee, Dr. Bronson was granted permission to establish a hospital [256]in Middlebury. The following advertisement appeared in *The Connecticut Journal,* published in New Haven, on September 18, 1792.

---

254 AND, p. 455.
255 Ibid.
256 This became known as the "Poxe House" or "Pest House."

INOCULATION

Any person desirous of taking the infection of the Small Pox, may be well accommodated by applying to the subscriber, who has a very convenient house for that purpose, where careful attendance is given, and every favor gratefully acknowledged, by their humble servant.

Abel Bronson,

Waterbury, Sept. 18, 1792   **10W.**

This house may have been located on Mirey Dam Road, near to where his own house stood, near the intersection of Mirey Dam and Burr Hall Roads. Anderson relates that a wooden door from this so-called "pest house," etched with the names of patients treated there, was removed to a house occupied by the late Burritt Hall. The door is currently in the possession of the Middlebury Historical Society. A second door is reportedly a part of the Mattatuck Museum collection.

Names inscribed thereon include: *"Sheldon, Malary, Ezekiel Birdsey, Sam'l D. H., Huntington, April 24, 1792; Jared Munson, Harry Edwards, Richard Skinner, Alfred Edwards, Samuel Wheeler, John Newton, of Washington, 1795; H. Marshall, Asa Green, Macomber Allis, Johnson, 23; Samuel Southmayd, Jr., Hodly, Clark, Sheldon Clark, Leavit T. Harris, and John Gilchrist."* Also included are the two sons of Nathaniel Gunn, of the Gunntown section of Middlebury, named Enos and Abel, who both died of exposure.

Assuredly, many others took the inoculation and, in all probability, a number of them died. There is no evidence that they were buried on the "pest house" property but, in the author's opinion, were likely interred in the Burying Ground at the foot of Breakneck Hill, to which we have referred earlier. Since that cemetery was later abandoned, in all likelihood the old pine "pest house" portal is the only remaining epitaph for the Gunn brothers and many more of these early settlers.

One of two original doors of Dr. Abel Bronson's Poxe House on Mirey Dam Road

**Just some of the many inscriptions carved by patients
of Dr. Bronson upon the Poxe House door**

Chapter XIII

Religious independence

The beginnings of religion in the West Farms of Mattatuck plantation did not reflect the puritanical intolerance seen in much of the remainder of New England. Rather, it assumed the open-mindedness and forbearance of Connecticut's founding fathers, such as the Rev. Thomas Hooker, who settled Suckiag [Hartford] in 1636. From Hartford, his magnanimity spread to the founding of Farmington in 1638 and, from thence to Mattatuck by 1658.

The founding of these early settlements rested upon three basic principles, as described in the Fundamental Orders:

First, the choice of public magistrates belongs to the people by God's own allowance.

Second, the privilege of election must be exercised according to the will and law of God, and;

Those who have the power to appoint officers and magistrates have also the power to set bounds and limitations on the power – because the foundation of authority is laid in the free consent of the people. [257]

Yet, Mattatuck's, now Waterbury's, first Society was very possessive of its membership, many of whom resided in outlying areas, such as present day Middlebury [West Farms], Watertown [Westbury] and Wolcott [Farmingbury], while at the same time maintaining its catholicity towards its early Episcopalian settlers.

In May of 1757, some thirty-three settlers of West Farms and "contiguous parts of Westbury [Watertown] Oxford, Southbury and the

---

257 BRD, p. 77.

old society of Woodbery" petitioned the General Court of the Colony at Hartford for "Winter Privileges," that is, the ability to hold services at some central place closer to their homes, thus avoiding the "sufferings endured in reaching places of public worship because of distance and the badness of the roads." [258] Some say the original petition, or "memorial" as they then called it, may have been submitted to the Court as early as 1731 but there is no evidence of this in the historical record. [259] Those who appended their names to the 1757 "peticion," included four Bronsons, Isaac, Isaac Jr., James and Josiah; two Benhams, Japhet and his son, Japhet Jr.; Two Weeds, John and Andrew; John and Amos Scott; Ebenezer and Edward Smith; Thomas and Gideon Mallary; as well as many other names who figured prominently in the early settlement of West Farms. These included Stephen Miles, James Burges(s), Daniel Tyler, Benjamin Bristol; Ezekial Tuttle; Arah Ward; Ebenezer Pender (?Porter); Reuben Hale; Noah Cande; Daniel Hawkins; [Dr.] Peter Powers; Abner Munson; Samuel Sherman; Stephen Abbott; Nathaniel Richardson and Thomas Masters. Two names on the original petition were illegible, while one signatory, Ebinezer Porter, was left out of the original area encompassed by the petition. [260]

The reader may recognize a number of these original signatories as giving their names to several places and roads in the Middlebury of today. Of the original thirty-three "memorialists," as they were then called, twenty-one lived in the west farms of Waterbury, of which fourteen belonged to the first society. They pleaded that most of them lived some five to six miles, and the nearest at least three miles, from any place of worship and it was extremely difficult for them "to attend the worship of God." Dr. Bronson points out that, in order to get to the Waterbury meeting house, attendance at services meant traveling the rough Woodbury road and fording the oft-times ice-filled river now called the Naugatuck. Nonetheless, with the Waterbury society's strong opposition, through a formal document called a remonstrance, the petition of 1757 was denied.

Waterbury's first society had much to lose. Tax monies and tithes, obligatory manual assistance – and the fact that similar groups of settlers in the other outlying areas were seeking similar privileges – would have the effect of diminishing the size of Waterbury's congregation considerably.

---

258 BRH, p. 276.
259 Personal Communication of Rev. Dennis Calhoun, former Pastor of the
    Middlebury Congregational Church, dated 3 Feb 1999.
260 Ibid. p. 277.

At the May session of the General Court three years hence, (1760) the memorial (petition) was re-entered this time with a request for full parish privileges. [261] The first society in Waterbury sent the General Court another "remonstrance," again arguing that such privileges would reduce significantly the amount of tax monies it collected from twenty-one "taxable persons" living there in West Farms. They represented a total of £1,282, 6s. on the Grand List. These "taxable persons," listed by Dr. Bronson, included James, Josiah, Isaac and Isaac Bronson Jr., Nathaniel, Ebinezer and Thomas Richa [rd] son, Amos, John, Edmund and Eunice Scott, (yes, a woman!) Ephraim Bissel, Dr. Peter Powers, Thomas Mallory, Benjamin Bristol, Stephen and David Miles, Ebinezer Lawton and Abner Munson. [262]

The citizens of Farmingbury, to the east, [263] had also petitioned the Court for similar privileges at the October meeting in the same year. "The effect would be to cut us up into mouthfuls ready for the devourer," [264] Waterbury argued. The resulting conclusion was that both petitions would yet again be denied. Another petition met the same fate, this time filed by fifty-four "memorialists" (petitioners) in May of 1761. [265]

At long last, still another Petition to the General Assembly, presented at the May session of the Court in 1786 was granted, but only in part, such that Winter Privileges were allowed "from the first day of December to the last day of March, annually, for three years." That same order set out the boundaries of what was to become present-day Middlebury, to wit: "Eight Mile Brook, Quassapaug pond, Israel Curtise's lot of mowing meadow land, the lane by Eliphat Bristol's running to Lt. Samuel Wheeler's, the saw mill on Hop brook, and a large rock with a number of pine trees on it, east of Ebenezer Richardson's." These bounds are roughly equivalent to the current bounds of the Town of Middlebury. For example, the "large rock" noted above, is the southernmost end of Two and a Half Mile Hill, (the hill running along the east side of Straits Turnpike) which was later called "Pine Rock," and around which, the old Middlebury road and trolley tracks ran, from Waterbury. This was before the Middlebury Road was rerouted through the "rock cut" just before its intersection with Straits Turnpike, formerly the Moss [Moses] road towards Watertown.

---

261 Ibid.
262 Ibid. p. 278.
263 Present-day Wolcott.
264 BRH, p. 277.
265 Ibid. p. 278.

The old society of Waterbury agreed to pay for preaching on eight Sabbaths during those ensuing winter months of that year. In the following year of 1787, Waterbury appropriated nine pounds for the same. By Dec. 29, 1790, the remonstrance of the old society of Waterbury had far less of an effect upon the General Court and the West Farms, together with adjoining portions of Woodbury and Southbury (Watertown had been made a separate society in 1780), which included thirty-five original families, were formed into a separate Ecclesiastical society under the name of Middlebury. [266] Just over a month later, in 1791, the Middlebury Ecclesiastical Society was formally established. There was, however, no church. Thus, Charles H. Upson, Selectman of the Town of Middlebury tells us, in his reflection at the 150th Anniversary celebration of the town in 1946, "from 1790 until 1807 – seventeen years – the Ecclesiastical Society of Middlebury was the church (parish) and the Town of Middlebury; its officers ran both the church and the Town."

Middlebury's "Church of Christ," presently Middlebury's Congregational Church, was organized and its Articles of Faith and Covenant were adopted at its founding on February 10, 1796. [267] Initially, there were twelve charter members, six of whom bore the name of Bronson and, quite surprisingly, two of whom were women. Seth Bronson and Nathan Osborn were elected the first Deacons. [268] There were ten Articles of Faith, asserting a belief in one true God, the writings of the Old and New Testaments, man's fall from grace, innate depravity, salvation through Jesus Christ and other tenets of Calvinism.

A profession of belief in these Articles was followed by the Covenant. "You do now solemnly, before God, angels and men, profess to choose God the Father, God the Son, and God the Holy Ghost to be your God," the Covenant read. And it continued: "And moreover, you acknowledge this church to be a real church of Christ, and do bind yourself, God's grace assisting... so long as God in his Providence shall continue you here." The Church promises, in return, that "through the grace of Christ, without whom we also can do nothing, we will walk towards you in all helpfulness, watchfulness and brotherly love."

In point of fact, three years earlier, construction had begun on Middlebury's first meeting house, located near the center of the west side of the present Green (then known as the "town park") It was the center

---

266 BRD, p. 73.
267 BRH, p. 280.
268 AND, p. 494.

of both church and civic life. Forty-one names appeared on the list of generous donors, who provided contractors' materials, monies or in kind services. The main entrance faced what is now South Street and the bell was forged in New York State, floated down the Hudson and into New Haven, from whence it was hauled by ox cart to its place in Middlebury history. The bell is incorporated into the present church structure. The great stone steps were cut from Mine Hill in Roxbury and carted overland on stone-bolt.

The cornerstone was laid on June 4, 1792 and also remains incorporated into the present church building. The interior of the original church exhibited a wide aisle to the center, galleries on three sides and no source of heat. Parishioners often wore heavy coats in winter and carried heated footstones to services, which were day-long, broken only by a Sabbath-day repast at noon (or nooning) in a small building called the Sabba [th]-day house, where the town hall now stands. The morning sermon often lasted two hours. Delia Bronson tells us that the front pews were reserved for the aged and the deaf. The tithingman, an elected position, would prod those who would dare to fall asleep during the sermon, with a long pole. He also had the duty of passing the plate or charger, hence the origin of the idea of "charging" admission. The church's first minister, Rev. Ira Hart, was installed in 1798 but, for some undisclosed reason, he was dismissed and replaced by Rev. Mark Reed on April 5, 1809.

The last service in the original church was held on Apr. 24, 1840, after which it was rebuilt on the present site, incorporating many of the original materials.[269]

As was said earlier, Middlebury became a village of great tolerance and charity. As early as 1786, West Farms Episcopalians organized themselves into the Gunntown parish, in the southwest part of the present town and in 1803 construction began on a small church there but was soon abandoned. Later, a Methodist Episcopal Society would be established near the present Green and the society's building still remains, across the street from Town Hall, as part of the Westover School. We will discuss the beginnings of Methodism in West Farms in Chapter XV.

---

269 BRD, p. 79-79.

Chapter XIV.

Breakneck's Oldest Resident

This unusual denizen of the Breakneck area has inhabited the north west corner of the junction of Breakneck Hill and Artillery Roads for perhaps two centuries. No one knows its origins. Nor is it likely a native species. But one thing is for certain. It is the largest of its kind in the entire state of Connecticut!

This unusual species is known in the scientific community as *Magnolia acuminata,* or in plain English, the Cucumber Magnolia. Named for its cucumber-shaped, immature fruit, which follow upon the loss of its early spring blossoms, the Middlebury specimen has a circumference of 206 inches. (Over 17 feet!)

Middlebury's state champion tree is 91 feet tall and, when fully leafed out, measures 70 feet in diameter across its spread. This greatest of Middlebury's trees was nominated for its lofty position by Peter North on January 1, 1989 and confirmed on November 20, 2000. [270]

Also known as the Cucumbertree (often expressed as a single word) or Blue Magnolia, this tree is native to the Appalachian belt. However, because of its cold-hardiness, it is now found in almost every state of the union. Although the young fruits are green, they gradually turn pinkish and eventually a dark red. The national champion of this species resides in Stark County, Ohio and is more than 7 feet, not in circumference, but in diameter. Yet it is only 79 feet tall.

So what of the origins of Middlebury's Cucumbertree? For one thing, it is obvious that it was planted on that corner. It lay directly across the road

---

270 See Website: http://oak.conncoll.edu:8080/notabletrees/

from where young Titus Bronson Jr. grew up. From Chapter IV, page 39, we learned that Titus travelled extensively in Michigan, Iowa and Illinois. Could he have passed trough Stark County, Ohio as well, carrying a young sapling home with him, as he returned to Breakneck in 1863? Whatever its origin, this Connecticut State Champion tree has withstood the test of time and will no doubt remain for many years into the future.

Flower of the Cucumber Magnolia. The Breakneck specimen is the largest in the State of Connecticut. (R. Sullivan photo)

Chapter XV.

A Church at Breakneck?

Some time before 1786, the Methodism of John Wesley and George Whitefield was beginning to take hold in the East Farms of Waterbury. Although Wesley was known for an evangelistic revival in the Anglican church, Whitefield was more Calvinistic. He preferred an unorthodox ministry of itinerant, open-air preaching. He spoke to the enslaved, indentured and impoverished; this, despite the fact that he was an ardent supporter of slavery. Through a practical, rather than dogmatic, approach to religion (and hence the moniker of "Methodism") Whitefield preached to the common man. Many became disillusioned with the rather stiff, puritanical approach to the Biblical teachings of the Congregationalists and Anglicans. Itinerant preaching became commonplace.

Those same itinerant preachers, who found fertile ground for their seeds of a new religion in the East Farms section of Waterbury, also planted Methodism in that part of the town, which, in 1807, became a part of Middlebury. Anderson tells us that the earliest of these preaching places was the home of Daniel Abbott, in the Breakneck district. [271] This house was located on the northwest corner of Breakneck Hill and the Wongum (Watertown) roads, opposite the Breakneck school.

Abbott was reportedly the leader of the first "class," in this area, a term commonly applied to a Methodist congregation. He was also the first male member of this "class." His puritanical old grandmother, Hannah, at 103 years of age, is said to have called her grandson a "Methodrate." To be a Methodist was, in her mind, nothing short of being a reprobate. Despite

271 AND, Vol. 3, p. 698.

this admonition, Daniel's "commodious kitchen of their farmhouse became a Methodist meeting-place and their home a well-known Methodist headquarters for many years." [272]

In 1786, Sarah Tyler, daughter of James C. Tyler, who lived just a short distance up Breakneck Hill Road, was married to Daniel's son, David. After three yeas of being exposed to the preaching of itinerants in her new home upon each Sabbath, Sarah fell victim to the preaching of one Peter Van Ness, a most popular itinerant of the day. "How can I forsake his ministry?" she asked of her Congregationalist father. Further, she would have to face the wrath of her even more conservative and extremely puritanical brother, Bennett, a protestant minister in his own right. "His word has awakened my soul," she pleaded. "What shall I do?" Her father's response was prompt and brief – "Thank him and let him go!" [273]

Perhaps out of guilt and continued family pressure, Sarah aligned herself with Middlebury's new congregational church but she continued to attend meetings of the local Methodists in her home. Her membership in the church on Middlebury's town park continued for some fifteen years but she was unimpressed with its old-school protestant ways.

Other itinerant Methodist preachers would influence her along the way – names such as Gad Smith and Benjamin Griffen would become the center of weekday talk in the Abbott home, for down-to-earth sermons and simple concepts of life. The weekly gatherings there at Breakneck would draw more and more individuals from present-day Middlebury and surrounds to the "class." Sarah would ultimately be converted under the powerful and charismatic preaching of Laban Clark. [274]

At last, by 1812/13 Sarah had had enough of the Congregational ways. In January of 1813, she would request a formal dismissal from the Congregational church. A committee of church elders promptly appeared on her doorstep, consisting of Deacon Seth Bronson, Aaron Benedict, Daniel Wooster and her neighbors to the west, Titus and Roswell Bronson. They listened to her reasons for requesting leave and took notes. Amongst those reasons were the fact that it was inconvenient for her to attend services at the centre; after all, Methodist meetings were held in her house. Methodist doctrines were more agreeable to her feelings and to her understanding of the Bible; there was more love and zeal in the preacher's words and amongst the "class." Sarah took no offense towards the Congregationalists

272 Ibid.
273 Ibid.
274 Ibid. p. 699.

but wished to simply "go away in charity with the church and have no hard feelings on either side."

Needless to say, her dismissal was refused. Formal charges of abandonment were levied against Sarah for "violation of the covenant obligations in absenting herself from the communion of this church and joining to another denomination." [275] These words are vaguely reminiscent of those spoken before the Massachusetts Bay Colony hung Mary Dyer for becoming a Quaker in the 1650s.

When called before the congregation as a whole, to answer to these charges, the strong-willed Mrs. Abbott refused to appear in person but rather chose to send a formal communication of withdrawal. When the vote was taken, by the Rev. Mark Mead, the pastor, Titus and Roswell Bronson voted contrary to the congregation's desire for formal withdrawal. But the "ayes" would prevail, thus agreeing to "withdraw our watch and fellowship from her, agreeable to the apostolic direction." [276]

It is of interest that one member of the committee on visitation, namely Daniel Wooster, became a Methodist himself and later became a prominent preacher of Methodism in his own right, in Middlebury and surrounding towns.

As for Sarah, she died in the Methodist faith on July 14, 1855, having left a considerable legacy to that church. The Abbott's daughters, Anna and Sarah remained devout Methodists, while their brothers, Ira and Alvin became Methodist preachers.[277] Furthermore, four grandchildren of Sarah and David Abbott became Methodist preachers of the New York East conference, themselves: quite a legacy for the little home in breakneck, where once, the concept of love of fellow man and a zeal for the holy life was first preached in Middlebury.

It is therefore most fitting, as Dr. Anderson relates, "the difficulties which the 'disorderly' Sarah Tyler Abbott encountered in becoming a Methodist and the influences which emanated from the old headquarters at Breakneck should find prominence in the annals of Waterbury Methodism." [278]

But the history of Abbots at Breakneck did not end with David and Sarah. Their son, Ira, began his Methodist ministry in 1839 and was pastor of the Waterbury church. In 1875, he retired to the old homestead on the

---

275 Ibid.
276 Ibid p. 700
277 Ibid.
278 Ibid. p. 701.

corner of the Watertown Road and Breakneck Hill. He died in the very house, in which he was born, April 15, 1883, at age seventy-one years. [279]

By 1824, some time after the incorporation of the Town, the Methodists moved their weekly "class" into an upper room of the old Union Academy, which they shared with the Episcopal Society and, by 1832 had built a church of their own, located next door. This Methodist church was eventually purchased by the Westover School and converted into a library. David Abbott unfortunately died in November of 1826 and, unlike his dear wife Sarah, never lived long enough to see the realization of his church.

---

279 Ibid, p. 700

Chapter XVI.

The Turnpike Comes Thru West Farms

In the 18th century, the name "pike" was employed to describe any route terminating at a specific point. Along the route, it was marked by a series of "turnstiles," consisting of four crossed bars, sharpened at their ends and turning on a center axle. In this way, one could control the passage of individuals, carts and wagons, by charging a fee or "toll" for passage through it in order to make use of the road.

In October of 1797, the Straits Turnpike Company was incorporated. [280] Some sixty years earlier, a portion of the route was called "the Straits" and as a result the name stuck. The first meeting of the newly formed corporation was held at the home of Irijah Terrill in Waterbury. The proposed route would have taken the new turnpike from the Litchfield Courthouse to the New Haven courthouse. There was much controversy over the fact that this route did not pass through the center of Waterbury town. Instead, it was voted to run the route through the westerly part of New Haven, through Westville, Amity and on a narrow gap in the mountains towards the Salem Society (present-day Naugatuck). The Route crossed a bridge over the Mattatuck (Naugatuck) River there and proceeded towards West Farms and the Westbury Society. (Present-day Watertown) From there, it took a fairly straight run to Litchfield. Waterbury was left out of the route. Some say Aaron Benedict, a prominent businessman of the time and a decorated officer in the Revolution, had considerable influence over the choice of routing the turnpike further west of Waterbury. Perhaps,

---

280 Ibid. p. 566.

the fact that his home was located at the corner of Park Road and the present Straits Turnpike had something to do with his position.

By 1761, the bridge across the Naugatuck had become a toll bridge, in order to provide the much needed funds to maintain it. The Salem Bridge soon became a bone of contention between the Turnpike Corporation and the town of Waterbury. Several bridges washed away but the corporation refused to rebuild, despite the fact that it was continuing to collect tolls. Claiming the cause of the last washout was a dike the corporation had built along the river to protect lowlands in present-day Union City, the town of Waterbury sued but to no avail. The town ended up paying the costs of rebuilding.

Interestingly, in May of 1806, the corporation secured from the General Assembly the right to erect houses at its gates. This applied to the gate at the Salem Bridge as well.

There is no evidence that such a "gate house" existed in Middlebury but the route through the town was altered to remove the large curve in the Mount Fair section of Middlebury as it approached Breakneck. (Now Kelly Road) The origin of the old Moss [Moses] Road near Nathaniel Richardson's tavern, originally located across Kelly Road, (the Old Woodbury Road) was eliminated in the process in what is now Route 63 as it left the junction of Route 64 on its way to Watertown. The old Straits Turnpike has subsequently been assigned the designation as state Route 63.

The turnpike did provide an efficient, smooth and rapid means of travel for West Farms residents, to and from New Haven and Litchfield. That is, assuming one could afford it! Anderson tells us that at each of the turnstiles along the route, a fare of 4 cents per person or horse was collected. For each chaise with one horse and passengers, 12 ½ cents was collected, while each four-wheeled pleasure carriage or stagecoach was levied 25 cents. [281]

The age of turnpikes ushered in the age of the tavern on a much larger scale. Prior to this time, there were several such establishments in the Breakneck area. Any house with an extra room and plenty of grog qualified as such. Innkeepers along the turnpike, in what is now Middlebury, were Samuel Judd and Stiles Thompson. The precise location of these taverns is unknown. [282]

---

281 Ibid. p. 567.
282 Ibid. p. 568.

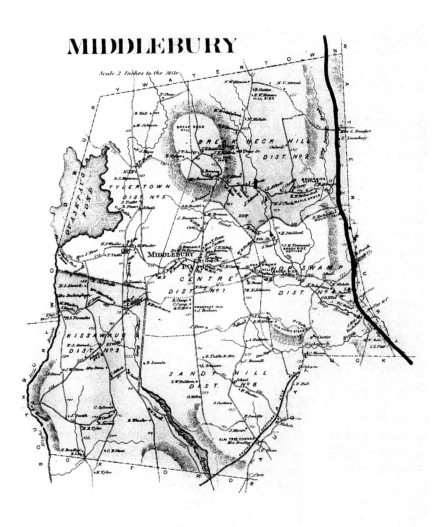

Fig. 3 - The Straits Turnpike alters somewhat the north-south route through West Farms in the 1790s.

Chapter XVII.

The Middlebury Society Becomes a Town

In June of 1800, Henry Bronson tells us, the society of Middlebury petitioned the General Assembly, that is, submitted a "memorial" for the passage of an Act, which would confer upon it the rights of an independent town. Waterbury opposed such an Act, as was anticipated but, this time, was not completely deaf to the request of Middlebury petitioners. Instead, the men of Waterbury appointed a committee to confer with them, to "hear their propositions," &c. [283] This committee consisted of Waterbury elders, Joseph Hopkins, Noah Baldwin and John Kingsbury.

Discussions must have gone on for several years, without any movement on either side. Therefore, in a further petition to the General Assembly of May 5, 1807 [284] requesting separation from Waterbury and incorporation as a separate town, it was pointed out to the Assembly that, by that date, about 175 families were included in the Middlebury society. One hundred eleven individuals signed the original petition. Eleven held the name of Bronson and four that of Porter. The petition elucidated the fact that Middlebury lay about six miles from the centre of each of the towns of Waterbury, Woodbury, Southbury, Watertown and Oxford. It also stated that Middlebury society was separated from Waterbury by a "rough and uninhabitable" tract of land. The Grand List for Middlebury was estimated at $20,960.67 – a sizeable sum. And this would have meant a considerable loss in revenue to the First Society in Waterbury. One can only imagine travelling the three miles of rough roads to Waterbury in harsh or rainy

---

283 BRH, p. 279.
284 AND, p. 495.

weather, to attend meetings of the First Society, only to face a return trip along those same rutted byways in the evening. Notification of the call to such meetings was likewise difficult.

In October of 1807, after numerous petitions (then called "remonstrances") from Waterbury in opposition to the formation of a separate town, the act of incorporation was finally obtained. Almost immediately, and in retaliation to this act, Waterbury voted *"to appropriate the monies awarded by the state committee in the affair of Waterbury against Middlebury ($600) as a perpetual fund for supporting a bridge across the Waterbury river."*[285] Waterbury would obtain its money from the inhabitants of Middlebury, one way or the other.

In the year 1807, the newly established government of the Town of Middlebury received the following document:

RESOLVE INCORPORATING THE TOWN OF MIDDLEBURY
PASSED OCTOBER, 1807

"Upon petition of Ebenezer Smith and others, inhabitants of the society Middlebury, composed of parts of the towns of Waterbury, Woodbury and Southbury.

RESOLVED BY THIS ASSEMBLY.

That the inhabitants living within the limits of said society of Middlebury be, and they hereby are, incorporated into and made a town by the name of "Middlebury," and that they and their successors forever, inhabitants within said limits, are and shall forever remain a town and body politic, with the rights, privileges and immunities to other towns belonging, excepting that they shall elect only one representative to the general assembly, and the lines and limits of said society shall be the lines and limits of said town of Middlebury; and the said town of Middlebury shall be liable for the support of their proportion of the poor of said towns, and of such as are now chargeable to said towns according to their list of August in the year 1806, and shall assume the maintenance thereof, and shall also pay their proportion of all the debts now due from said towns according to their list as aforesaid, and in case of any disagreement between said

---

285 Ibid.

towns in the matters aforesaid, it shall be referred to and settled by the committee hereinafter named.

And whereas, it is represented to this assembly that there will be left in said town of Waterbury to be supported more than a due proportion of bridges, it is resolved that Andrew Hull, rufus Hitchcock of Cheshire, Josiah Dudley of Derby and Merk Harrison of Wolcott, Esqs. or any three of them be, and they are hereby appointed a committee at the expense of said towns of Waterbury and Middlebury to examine said subject and to decide what sum shall be paid by said town of Middlebury to said town of Waterbury annually, or in gross by installments for the support of bridges as aforesaid, and to deduct there from if they judge proper, in part or in whole, the proportion of said society of Middlebury to the ministerial and school monies of said town of Waterbury, which moneys is relinquished by said Middlebury except as aforesaid, and said committee shall meet at Beecher's tavern in said Waterbury on the third Monday of December next, to attend the duty hereby assigned to them.

Said town of Middlebury shall hold their first town meeting at the meetinghouse in said Middlebury on the third Monday of November next, at 2 o'clock in the afternoon, to choose their town officers for the year ensuing, and said meeting shall be warned by posting a notification to that effect on the signpost in said Middlebury ten days before said third Monday of November, which notification shall be signed by Samuel W. Southmayd, Esq., who shall be the moderator of said town meeting, and in case the said Southmayd should fail to perform the duty hereby assigned to him, the same may be performed by any justice of the peace in any town adjoining said town of Middlebury.

And whereas, there are inhabitants of Waterbury, previous to this incorporation, who live without the limits of Waterbury and Middlebury, and hereafter may become chargeable without said limits, whenever said charge shall happen it shall be paid by said towns of Waterbury and Middlebury, according to the list of August, 1806." [286]

The committee thus appointed to settle differences between the surrounding towns regarding accounts, care of the poor, roads, bridges, etc. consisted of Messrs. Harrison, Hull and Hitchcock. They met at

---

286 Middlebury Land Records, V.1, Index Z.

Beecher's tavern – yes, a tavern - in Waterbury on the third Monday in December of that year of 1807.

"We the Subscribers, being by the Honorable General Assembly at their Session in October last, appointed a Committee to adjust and settle the differing claims which might arise between the Towns of Waterbury and Middlebury relative to the Town Accounts, the Poor o said Town and the due portion of roads and bridges et cetera, etc." [287]

Meanwhile, however, the town had already held its first meeting on Nov. 16th previous and elected its representative to that committee. The outcome of deliberations resulted in Middlebury's paying the sum of $40. to Waterbury, with no payments to Woodbury or Southbury. It was also agreed for Middlebury to purchase all the roads and bridges, existing in the town, from Waterbury for an additional $600. to be paid in six installments without interest. [288]

The following Town Officers were elected at the first Town Meeting:

Town Clerk: Larmon Townsend
Selectmen: Eli Bronson, Aaron Benedict and Ephram Tuttle.
Treasurer/Clerk: Larmon Townsend.
Constables: Stiles Thompson and Amos Benham.
Surveyors of Highways: John Bradley, Hezekiah Clark, Daniel Smith, Isaac Riggs, Eli Hine, Job Wheeler, Roswell Tyler, Caleb Munson, Jr., Eli Thompson, Daniel Saxton, Philo Bronson, Abel Bronson, Daniel Wooster, Augustus Peck, Asa Fenn.
Listers: Nathaniel Richardson, Asahel Bronson, Isaac Riggs, Theophilies Baldwin and Ezekial Stone.
Grand Jurors: Aaron Tuttle, Titus Bronson and EbenezerRichardson.
Fence Viewers: Jonothon Sanford and Hezekiah Clark.
Sealer of Weights and Measures, Key-keeper: John Bradley.
Collector of Taxes: Stiles Thompson.
Town Agent: Aaron Benedict.

In addition, a committee was selected to "settle with the several towns." This included Ephraim Tuttle, Eli Bronson, Aaron Benedict, John Stone, Simeon Manville, Daniel Smith and Eli Hine.

The reader will immediately recognize many of these names as already appearing in previous chapters in this book.

---

287 Middlebury Town records, V.1, pp.1-2.
288 BRD, p. 74.

At the second Town Meeting, held one week after the first, on November 23rd, Isaac Bronson was chosen Moderator and Asa Fenn was chosen as Highway Surveyor. Rev. Dennis Calhoun, former pastor of the Middlebury Congregational Church, directed the author to a humorous note in the Minutes of that meeting:

"Voted that the Selectmen be empowered to borrow a sum not Exceeding Sixty Dollars to defray the Exigencies of the Town until we tax ourselves..."

Rev. Caloun is quick to point out that, from the above on can see that "deficit spending has a long history!" [289] In the minutes of the same meeting, he also notes:

Voted that Swine, if a ring in their Nose, be free commoners (Excepting Boars) for the year ensuing."

In other words, pigs with rings in their noses were granted the same legal status for the ensuing year as non Congregationalists held and were free to come and go as they pleased!

At the third meeting of the Town of Middlebury, held on February 1, 1808, the townspeople voted to levy the tax previously mentioned, at a rate of "three cents laid on the Dollar on the List of 1807." By the Author's calculations, this would have raised approximately $629.00, or enough to cover the debts owed to Waterbury. Ephraim Tuttle was charged with the collection of the tax, for which he would be paid the grand sum of ten dollars.

One year later, on April 11, 1808, the inhabitants gathered at the Meeting House and voted unanimously (sixty-six votes) to join to the New Haven County as opposed to Litchfield County. The manner of voting was quite interesting.

"Resolved that those who shall prefer that the said Town of Middlebury be permanently affixed to the County of New Haven pass to the right of the Moderator and those who prefer that the same be set to the County of Litchfield pass to the left." [290]

Captain Isaac Bronson of Breakneck was appointed agent, at the same meeting, in behalf of the Town "to represent the sense thereof as expressed in the above vote of said Meeting to the Hon'd. General Assembly...on the 2nd Thursday of May."

289 Calhoun, Rev. Dennis B.: *From the Meeting House to the Town Hall,* a sermon delivered to his Congregation, 15 Apr. 1994, In possession of the Author.
290 Middlebury Town Records, V.1, p. 8

Another interesting event occurred at the September meeting of the townspeople. In December of 1807, in response to the firing upon and boarding of the USS Chesapeake, off the coast of Norfolk, Virginia, and the murder, wounding and impressment of American sailors by the British, Congress voted to establish the Embargo Act of 1807. Under this Act, all trade between the United States and other nations was banned during the Napoleonic wars. Such an embargo had a profound effect on the business of trade in major ports all along the eastern seaboard. New Haven was no less affected and its citizens, most of who depended on trade, in dire need.

Further, in March 1808, Congress banned all exports, either by land or by sea, to any foreign power. The Act also imposed heavy fines upon violators and gave port authorities broad powers including the ability to search and seize ships without a warrant. For the port towns, this was just too much.

On September 19th, 1808, a committee was appointed to prepare a Petition to the President of the United States, then Thomas Jefferson, to wit:

"To Thomas Jefferson, President of the United States –
The Memorial of the Inhabitants of the Town of Middlebury in the County of New Haven & State of Connecticut in legal Town Meeting assembled – Respectfully sheweth that your Memorialists being involved in common with the Citizens of New Haven in the various Embarrassments and privations incurred by the Embargo Laws as set forth in the Petition of the Town of New Haven bearing date 29th August 1808 and being impressed with a sense of the evils there complained of so concur with them in the Memorial of said Town and do unite our prayers with them that in pursuance of the powers vested in the President of the United States by an Act of Congress for that purpose... the operation of the several Laws imposing an Embargo may be Immediately suspended." [291]

The ban was at long last lifted in 1809, after numerous such "Memorials" directed to President Jefferson. It occurred just three days before he left office. It was replaced by the Non-intercourse Act, which restricted the trade embargo to Britain and France.

In 1809, the position of Town Grave-digger was established but we have no knowledge of the first to hold this office. The first tax of 3 mills was enacted on Feb. 1, 1808. In May of that year, Capt. Isaac Bronson rode

---

291 Ibid. p. 9.

to Hartford on horseback, to announce the town's preference to join to New Haven County over Litchfield County, by unanimous vote. In order to make up a deficit, (just as continues today) a second levy of 2 mills was collected in November of that year. But, by April of the year following, the selectmen were frugal enough to reduce taxes to a rate of only 1 ½ mills. Perhaps a lesson can be learned from our past.

****

In the year 1817, the following resolution regarding the annexation of another portion of Waterbury to the town of Middlebury was passed by the general assembly:

RESOLVE ANNEXING A PART OF WATERBURY TO THE TOWN AND SOCIETY OF MIDDLEBURY_ PASSED OCTOBER, 1817

RESOLVED BY THIS ASSEMBLY,

"That part of the town and society of Waterbury lying on the westerly side of a line beginning at a town monument 112 rods northward of Union bridge, so-called, and thence running south twenty-nine degrees, east three hundred and seventeen rods to Salem society line, and then west four degrees, north one hundred and twenty-three rods to an ancient monument between the towns of Waterbury and Middlebury, be, and the same is hereby, annexed to the town and society of Middlebury, and shall hereafter, to all legal purposes whatever, be deemed a part of the town and society of Middlebury, any law to the contrary notwithstanding."

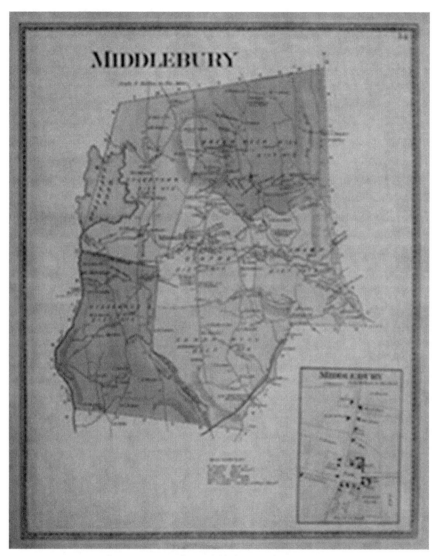

Figure 4 - A Map of Middlebury during the 1800s.

Thus, the eastern boundary of Middlebury is complete. A small projection of Waterbury's western boundary still exists as one travels south on Old Straits Turnpike, between Middlebury and Naugatuck. Northern bounds with Watertown, western bounds with Woodbury, Southbury and Oxford as well as southern bounds with Naugatuck remain set as in the original resolution of the General Assembly in October of 1807. Hence, the area once known as the West Farms of the Mattatuck Plantation, later Waterbury, and the tiny village once known as Breakneck, has evolved into what is today, the independent and beautiful Town of Middlebury, in the great State of Connecticut.

Over the centuries since Isaac Bronson The Planter chose to build his first house on the north side of the "woodbery road" at Breakneck, the town has changed little. It still remains a "bedroom" community of Waterbury, to which it once belonged, and aside from an amusement park and a few larger corporate headquarters buildings, the visitor will note few differences from the former agrarian nature of the town. For the most part, the farms are gone but one can still catch an occasional glimpse of cattle on Tucker Hill Road or the planted fields of "cow corn" along Route 188. Deer and wild turkey can still be seen frequently as one drives along the town's roads and the occasional cry of a Fisher cat is heard at Breakneck on a balmy July night. A Red-tailed Hawk can be frequently seen soaring overhead. The old trolley line is gone now, replaced with a lovely Greenway for walking or cycling. But homes such as that of Josiah Bronson remain since 1738, as vivid reminders of our illustrious past.

For those forgotten souls who reside in the rich, dark earth of Breakneck, it was a harsh yet wonderful place to have lived and grown; a place where countless younger generations have been able to tell their own children of the many pleasantries found there; where enticing stories abound, if one only takes the time to search for them, and where noteworthy history was created.

Appendix

Ancient Place Names

In order to better serve the reader, the author has chosen to include a final chapter on ancient place names, many of which may still be found within the confines of present-day Middlebury. Thanks in large measure to Dr. Joseph Anderson once again, many of these earliest place names, which figured prominently in locating homes and historic sites in what is now Middlebury have been preserved. Some of the names to which he refers are contemporaneous to his time and have all but disappeared. The following represent an update of his alphabetical listing in 1896:

ABBOTT'S POND - The Breakneck Hill Road, near the location of the first Breakneck School, crosses this small pond. It was originally known as Bronson's Pond, since Isaac Bronson Sr. built the dam to power the area's first sawmill, on a branch of the Hop Brook there.

BEDLAM BROOK – either what is now Long Meadow brook or a brook running into it.

BEDLAM HILL – The hill upon which the present center of Middlebury is located. "In 1784 there was a school-house on it." [292] It runs north south towards Naugatuck.

BEDLAM MEADOW – the area now covered by the man-made Long Meadow Pond, to the west of the southern end (Biscoe's hill) of Bedlam Hill.

---

292 This was the old Center School, presently the home of the Middlebury Historical Society

BIRCH HILL – later called Camp's hill, it lies southerly of Hop Swamp and was so named for the large stand of White Birch, which once covered it.

BISCOE'S HILL – is the southern end of Bedlam Hill. Named after Samuel Biscoe who moved there from Milford. On this hill, lies Biscoe's Farm, owned by the Larkin family.

BISSELL HILL – the long hill running east-west from Mount Fair to Yale Avenue along the northern edge of which the Middlebury road now runs, as one drives from Waterbury. The hill is so named for Ephraim Bissell, who came from Tolland in 1728, to build a house on the southern slope of this hill, overlooking Hop Swamp.

BISSEL'S SWAMP – This swamp is located at the southern end of Three Mile Hill. A stream feeding this swamp (a branch of the Hop Brook) now runs through a large culvert under the Memorial Middle School parking lot.

BRADLEYVILLE – This is the area along Hop Brook close to where the Hop Brook Recreation Area now lies. Several early factories and mills existed in this area, including the Bradley Knife Factory. Some may remember the White Stone food stand located in this region, along the old road to Naugatuck.

BREAK-NECK – This was the first settled area of present-day Middlebury, located to the east of Breakneck Hill and extending from that hill eastward to the area of Memorial Middle School.

BREAK-NECK HILL – This hill was named well before 1688, according to Waterbury town records. . The idea that it was named because an ox, hauling Rochambeau's artillery up that steep hill, broke its neck, as the result of the difficult climb, is simply not true. Breakneck hill is described as the long hill running north and south, from the area of Mirey Dam Road south to Charcoal Avenue. It is located about half way from Waterbury to Woodbury. Fenn's Farm is located just below the southernmost end of this hill.

BRONSON'S MEADOW – It is just one of many so-named, in the original Mattatuck plantation. The large "fair meadow-tract" between

Two-and-a-Half Mile Hill and Three Mile Hill, where Memorial Middle School now sits. The area was earlier known as Race Plain.

BRONSON'S BOGGY MEADOW – This tract takes its name from John Bronson in 1688. Though not fully determined, it is thought to be the swampy tract of land located between branches of Hop Brook, northwest of Three Mile Hill, and in the valley between it and Breakneck hill. .

BUNKER HILL ROAD – before 1720, it was known as the Upper Road to Woodbury and later re-named in honor of the famous revolutionary battle. It actually lies in Watertown and crosses the Watertown Road from Middlebury.

CEDAR SWAMP – This is the large swamp beginning in the northwest corner of Lake Quassapaug and extending towards Woodbury to the west and Watertown to the north. It is mentioned in an Indian deed of 1684.

EIGHT MILE BROOK – This is the brook which originates at the outlet of Lake Quassapaug, near the Woodbury line and flows southward to form the bounds with Woodbury and Southbury, then on into Oxford, where it joins the Housatonic River there. It is so named because it is approximately eight miles from its source to the Housatonic River.

GOAT BROOK – This brook takes its origins above Fenn's Farm, drains through the man-made Fenn's pond and crosses the Middlebury road near its outlet. It then runs along the Greenway to eventually join Hop Brook. Along this brook, roughly opposite the Convalescent home, one can see the remains of the foundation of an early mill. The origins of its name are unknown.

GREAT HILL EAST OF QUASSAPAUG – This hill runs north and south, rising above the eastern shore of the lake between it and what were once the Woodbury bounds, along Tranquility and Old Watertown Roads.

GUNNTOWN – This area, just north of the Millville section of Naugatuck, lies within the bounds of Middlebury, and was originally inhabited by Nathaniel Gunn, Sr. It was a part of a six acre land grant to Timothy Standly in 1687. It can be reached by driving south on South Street.

HIKCOX MEADOW BROOK – This name is sometimes applied to the north branch of Hop Brook as it lies in Middlebury.

HOP BROOK – This brook consists of two major branches passing through Middlebury, along with many smaller branches, coming together to flow into the Hop Brook Recreation Area towards Naugatuck. It is described by Anderson as rising: "east of Lake Quassapaug at an elevation of 750 feet above the sea, runs through Cedar Swamp northward of the lake and wavers through about fifteen miles of territory, receiving at least fifteen tributaries...." [293]It eventually enters the Naugatuck River in that town. The more western branch flows through Abbott's Pond, while the eastern branch flows across the Memorial Middle School parking lot, through a large culvert, and into Bissell's swamp, adjacent to Memorial Drive.

HOP SWAMP – the swampy area crossed by the Hop Brook in the region of the lower Whittemore Road, in the vicinity of the old Mary I. Johnson School. (Originally Hop Swamp School and now the offices of Region 15 Schools) So named for the abundance of wild hops, which grew in the area and were used in the making of beer.

MESHADDOCK – described as located in Middlebury, east of Bedlam Hill and north of Sandy Hill. The area through which Shadduck Road now runs, east of Sandy Hill Road. Apparently an early Native American name.

MOSS ROAD (or Moses Road) – "a former highway called Moss's road." The present town line between Middlebury and Naugatuck, in the southeast corner, is a portion of the Moss road. [294]Before Straits turnpike was built, this road served as a major route from the Salem Society (Naugatuck) to Westbury (Watertown). It ran along the old Nichols road (an existing dirt road) onto the northern part of Shadduck road to the area of Hop Swamp School (Region 15 offices). The road then extended northward from the Hop Swamp School, to Maple Drive, over the eastern end of Bissell hill, through Mount Fair and onto the present Kelly Road. Near Memorial school, it leaves Kelly Road to run towards the present Strait's Turnpike, which it predated. Remnants of the road may still be seen on the right, as one drives down the Turnpike towards its junction with the Middlebury road and just below Exit 17 west, from I-84.

MOUNT FAIR – This is the area of homes lying just south of the junction of Strait's Turnpike and the Middlebury Road. Remnants of the old road

---

293 AND, p. 353.
294 Ibid. p. 703.

from Waterbury may still be seen in the area, on the left, just opposite Rose Court, as one takes the Turnpike towards Naugatuck. The earliest settlers of the area may have named it.

PINE ROCK – This rock composes the southern end of Two-and-a-half Mile Hill, around which the old road and trolley track from Waterbury ran into Middlebury bounds, as it entered Mount Fair. In the early 1900's, a "little people's village" was created here as an attraction for trolley riders on the line to Woodbury. Named for a lonely Pine tree, which mounted its crest.

RACE PLAIN – the semi-level area lying between Three Mile Hill and Straits Turnpike. Also known as Bronson's Meadow.

SATAN'S MEDITATION – Originally a portion of the Miry [Mirey; Miery] Swamp located east of Mirey Dam road, this area lies between the branches of Hop Brook. The origin of the name is unknown.

THREE MILE HILL – This is the long hill running north and south, along which the Three Mile Hill road runs. It is so named because of its position just three miles from the old Waterbury center and not because of its length.

TOWANTIC – The area presently occupied by Long Meadow Pond was once called Towantick. Another early Native American name, which has persisted over the centuries. Also once known as Bedlam Meadow, it is a part of Gunntown. See above.

TWO-AND-A-HALF MILE HILL – This is the long hill running north and south from Park Road, along the present Strait's Turnpike and continuing across the Middlebury Road to Pine Rock. It too is so named because of its position two and a half miles from the old Waterbury center. It is now broken by the "rock cut" just off Exit 17 of I-84, heading west.

WONGUM ROAD [WAUGUM] – the present Watertown Road, beginning at Breakneck Hill Road, near what was once the Breakneck district school and running to Watertown. Also probably Native American in origin.

Abbreviations for References used in this Work

HPJ   Johnson, Henry P.: Record of Connecticut Men in Military and Naval Service during the Revolutionary War 1775 – 1783. Clearfield Publ., Hartford (1889)

WMC Cothren, William: History of Ancient Woodbury, Connecticut, From the First Indian Deed in 1659 to 1754. Reproduced by the Genealogical Publishing Co. Baltimore. 1977

CHS   Rolls and Lists of Connecticut Men in the Revolution, 1775 – 1783. Connecticut Historical Society, Albert C. Bates, Ed. Hartford, 1899-Vols. 7 –10.

CNP   Census of Pensioners for Revolutionary Military Services. Wash., D.C., 1841. (195 pp.)

AND   Anderson, Joseph, D.D., Ed.: The Town and City of Waterbury, Connecticut from the Aboriginal Period to the Year 1895. Price and Lee Co. New Haven, 1896.

KAP   Prichard, Katherine A.: Proprietors' Records of the Town of Waterbury Connecticut 1677-1761. Mattatuck Hist. Soc., Waterbury, CT, 1911.

PRD   Prichard, Katharine A.: Ancient Burying Grounds of Waterbury, Connecticut together with other Records of Church and Town. Vol. II, Publications of the Mattatuck Historical Society, 1917.

BRH   Bronson, Henry: The History of Waterbury, Connecticut; the Original Township Embracing Present Watertown and Plymouth, with Parts of Oxford, Wolcott and Middlebury, Prospect and Naugatuck, with an Appendix of Biography, Genealogy and Statistics. 1858.

SMB   Smith, Bradford E.: Middlebury, Connecticut Church and Vital Records 1775 – 1900. 1984.

HED   Heddon, James S.: Roster of Graves or of Monuments to Patriots of 1775 – 1783, and Soldiers of Colonial Wars in and Adjacent to New Haven County. 1934.

BRD   Bronson, Delia S.: History of Middlebury, Connecticut. Middlebury Historical Society, Inc. 1992.

DRS   Selig, Dr. Robert A.: Rochambeau in Connecticut: Tracing His Journey. Historical and Architectural Survey. Connecticut Historical Commission, (Connecticut) 1999.

ACB   Bates, Albert C., Ed.: Rolls of Connecticut Men in the French and Indian War, 1755 – 1762, 2 Vols CT Historical Soc. Hartford. 1903.

CWB   Burpee, Charles W.: The Military History of Waterbury, from the founding of the Settlement in 1678 to 1891… Price, Lee & Adkins Co., New Haven, 1891.

WMB   Beauchamp, Rev. W.M.: Revolutionary Soldiers resident or dying in Onondaga County, New York… Onondaga Historical Ass'n., Syracuse, 1913.

WAC   Cothren, William A.: A History of Ancient Woodbury From the First Indian Deed in 1659 to 1872 Including the Present Towns of Washington, Southbury, Bethlehem, Roxbury and Parts of Oxford and Middlebury. (2nd Ed.) Woodbury, CT, 1872.

RRH   Hinman, Royal R., Compiler: A Historical Collection from Official Records, Files, etc. of the Part Sustained by Connecticut during the War of Revolution. E. Gleason, Pub. Hartford, 1842.

WJP   Pape, William J.: A History of Waterbury and the Naugatuck Valley, Connecticut. S.J. Clark Pub. Co., Chicago-New York. 1918.

ORC   Orcutt, Samuel & Ambrose Beardsley: History of the Old Town of Derby, Connecticut. 1642 – 1880. Springfield Printing Co., Springfield. 1880.

END   Enderton, Col. Herbert Bronson, Compiler: Bronson (Brownson, Brunson) Families. Some Descendents of John, Richard and Mary Brownson of Hartford, Connecticut in 3 Vols, 1969.

WAL   Walwer, Gregory and Dorothy N.: Phase I Archaeological Reconnaissance and Phase II Archaeological Report of the Middlebury Golf Community in the Town of Middlebury, Connecticut. Special Collections, Thomas J. Dodd Research Library, University of Connecticut. November 2004.

Breinigsville, PA USA
08 November 2010
248906BV00001B/2/P